marie claire

table

acknowledgements

Karen Spresser
Many thanks to Jackie Frank for giving me the opportunity to write this book and to Kay Scarlett for commissioning me. It is a pleasure to see my words accompany Yael Grinham and John-Paul Urizar's beautiful images. I'd also like to thank Anna Waddington for keeping me organised and Marylouise Brammer for her wonderful design skills. Lastly, thank you to Neil, my wonderful husband, for his support and patience through it all, and to Thomas for helping me keep everything in perspective.

Yael Grinham
Thank you to Kate Hoskins for all your encouragement, cooking, sewing and friendship.

Many props were lent for this book. Thank you to Anibou, Australia on a Plate, Cloth, DIA, Domestic Pots, Empire Homeware, Freedom Furniture, IKEA, Kate Howard Ceramics, Ordal Australia, Organique Flowers by Michelle Cambridge, Orient House, Orrefors Kosta Boda, Orson & Blake, Parterre Gardens, Peppergreen in Berrima, Ruby Star Traders, Wheel & Barrow Homewares, and many friends and family.

This book contains information on some essential oils. Neither the author nor the publisher can be held responsible for any adverse reaction to the recommendations and instructions contained within this book.

marie claire

table

yael grinham & karen spresser
photography by john-paul urizar

MURDOCH
BOOKS

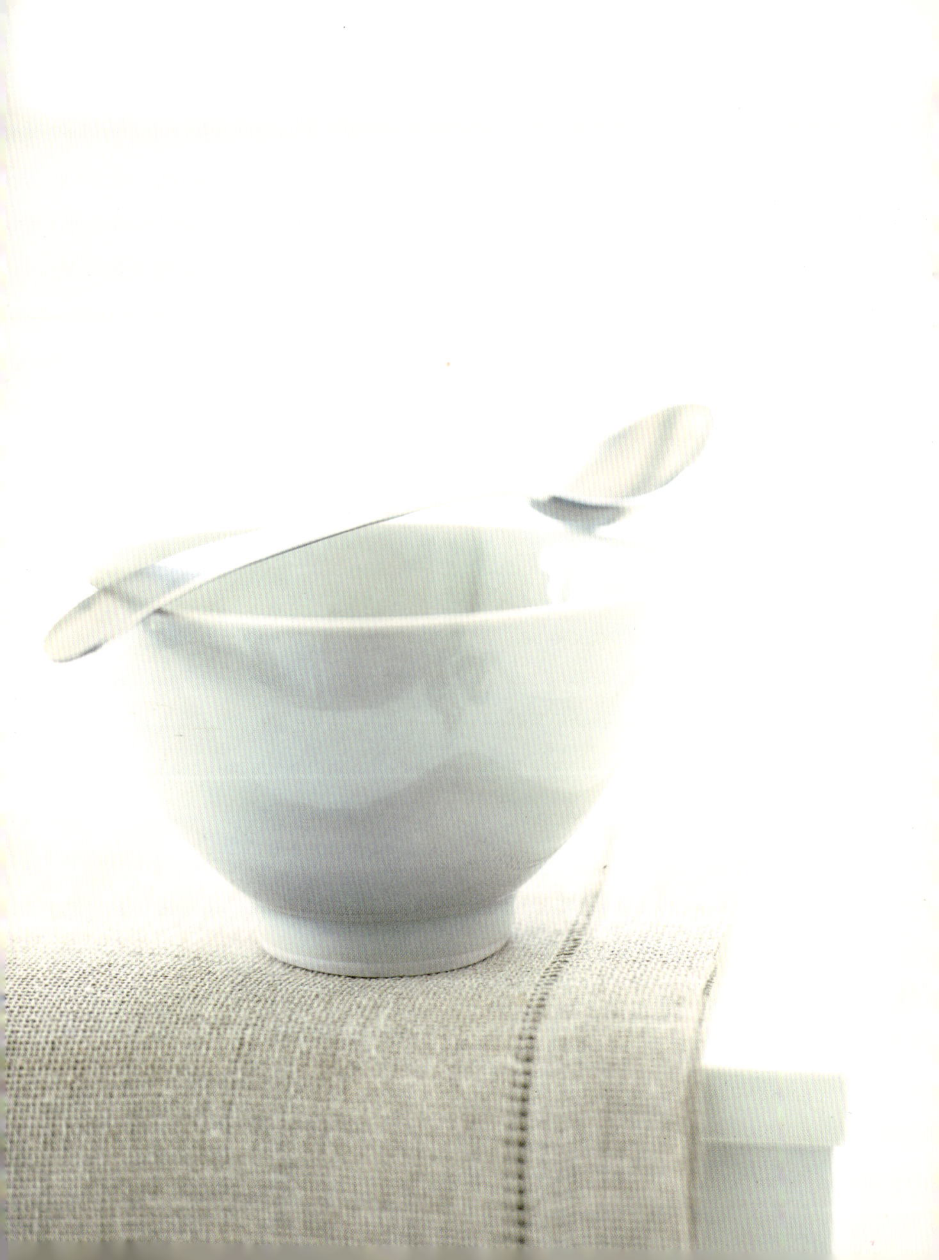

contents

introduction	6	winter	44
		dramatic times	46
summer	8	a place for everything	51
simply summer	10	scent from heaven	54
summer style	15	dining in style	59
fresh flowers	18	go for drama	60
cool ideas	23		
summer party	24	spring	62
		fresh, pretty, light	64
autumn	26	fruit flavoured	69
autumn colours	28	perfect picnic	72
autumn beauty	33	break from tradition	77
on the side	36	garden treasures	78
unusual touches	41		
special occasions	42		

introduction

The aim of this book is to give you ideas. To inspire you. To show how simple things can make a huge difference, and that table settings can be beautiful and imaginative, simple and stunning—and not cost a fortune. This book is full of options. It will show you how to turn the ordinary into the extraordinary. All it takes is a little time and effort, and a touch of inspiration. Harness what you already have and look at it in a new light. Use tables to display, to store, to delight. Make them comfortable, welcoming and joyful—tables that people want to sit and linger at while they enjoy mouthwatering food and good company. This book is divided into four chapters: summer, autumn, winter and spring. In each, seasonal accompaniments—plants, shells, candles, leaves, flowers, fruits—have been incorporated. Everyday objects are mixed with the unusual, the eclectic and the unexpected to create unique, timeless tables. Some are romantic, some are dramatic, some are simply gorgeous. All contain a wealth of fresh ideas that will bring a sense of occasion and beauty to any meal or any event.

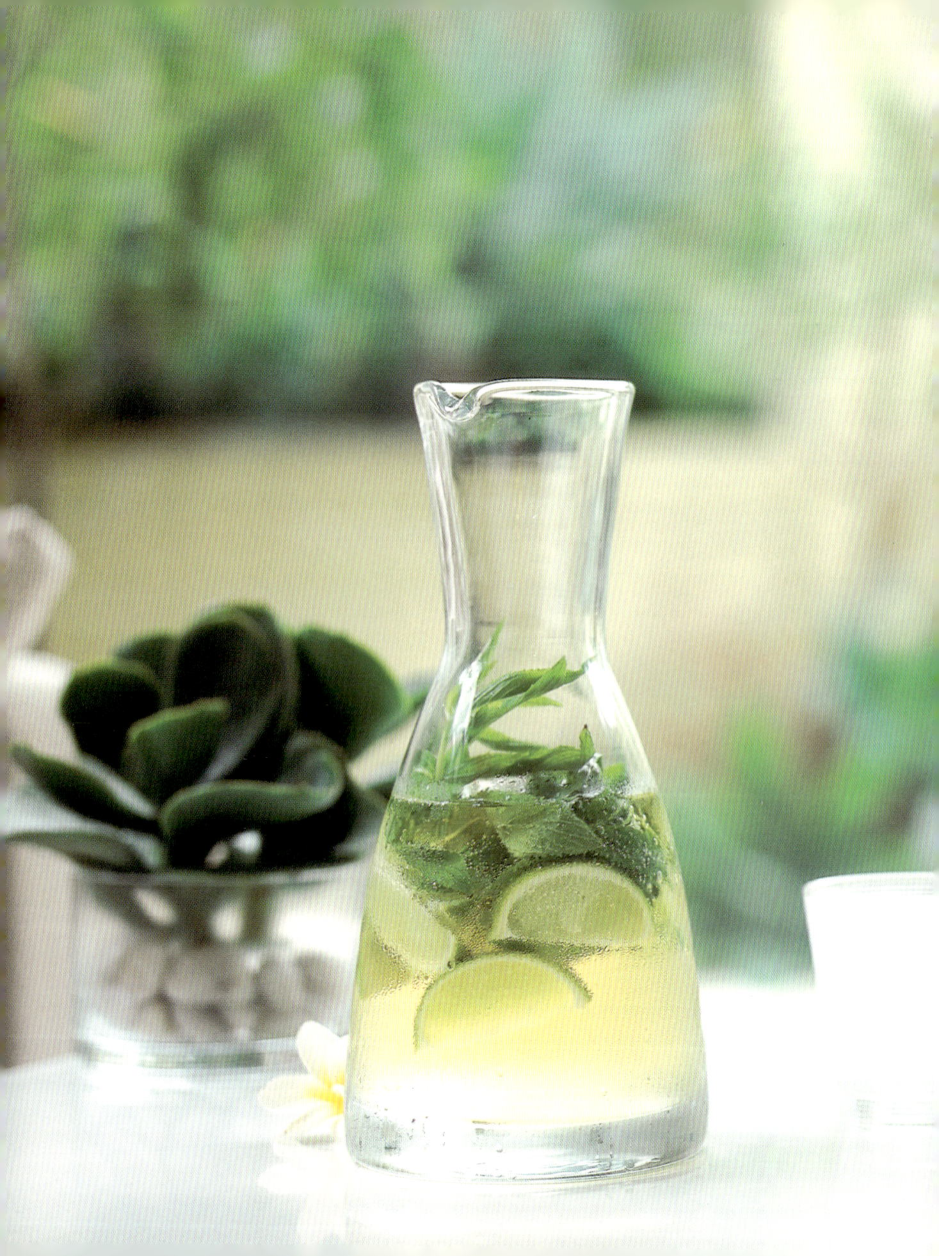

summer

simply summer

Summer is all about simplicity. Hot days and warm nights lend themselves to a laid-back, easier way of life. Nothing should look like it has taken too much time or effort. A lack of structure, even in formal surroundings, adds freshness, a sense of ease. Move outdoors where everything naturally takes on a more relaxed approach. Make the most of sunny days: take a picnic to the park, have brunch on the terrace, coffee by the beach, and, when the sun goes down, dinner under the stars. And let tables reflect that ease of living—fresh, simple, generous, luscious. Throw a colourful rug under a tree, move a side table and chairs out onto the balcony, cover the old barbecue table with a crisp linen cloth and invite friends around for a midsummer's night feast. Summer tables should be all about fresh produce, beautiful flowers and good times. And the setting should be the perfect backdrop. Elegant tables lend themselves to any meal—breakfast, lunch, dinner, or anything in between. Whether it's supper for two or a cook-out for 20, tables should reflect the mood and the food. Generous plates, gleaming cutlery, sparkling glasses and crisp napkins are the solid foundation. Add flowers, candles, ribbons, placemats, fruit and shells and you've elevated it from everyday ordinary to something special.

Dining outdoors is what summer is all about

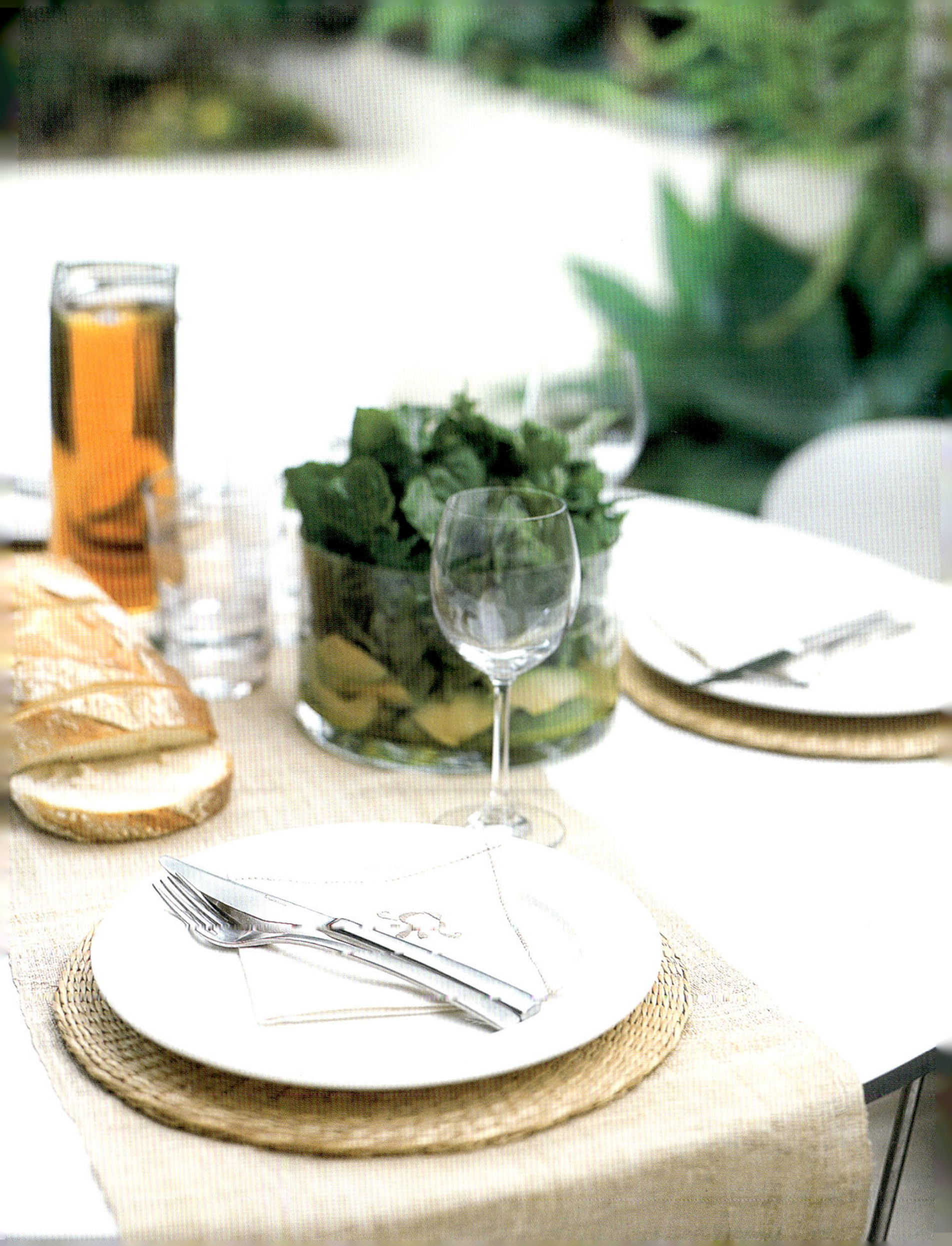

scent of summer
Use small, collectable bottles or jars instead of traditional vases. A spray of gardenias and a few sprigs of leaves look beautiful in an old milk bottle.

napkin ties
Interesting shells collected from the beach can be pasted with craft glue to a length of pretty ribbon, which is then used as a tie for napkins.

summer seasoning
Make interesting little pots from scallop, pipi, clam or mussel shells. Clean them well and use as containers to serve condiments or salt and pepper.

placemats
Gather green banana leaves to use as placemats. If you can't find banana leaves, use other large, flat leaves such as antherium, elephant's ear or ginger.

summer

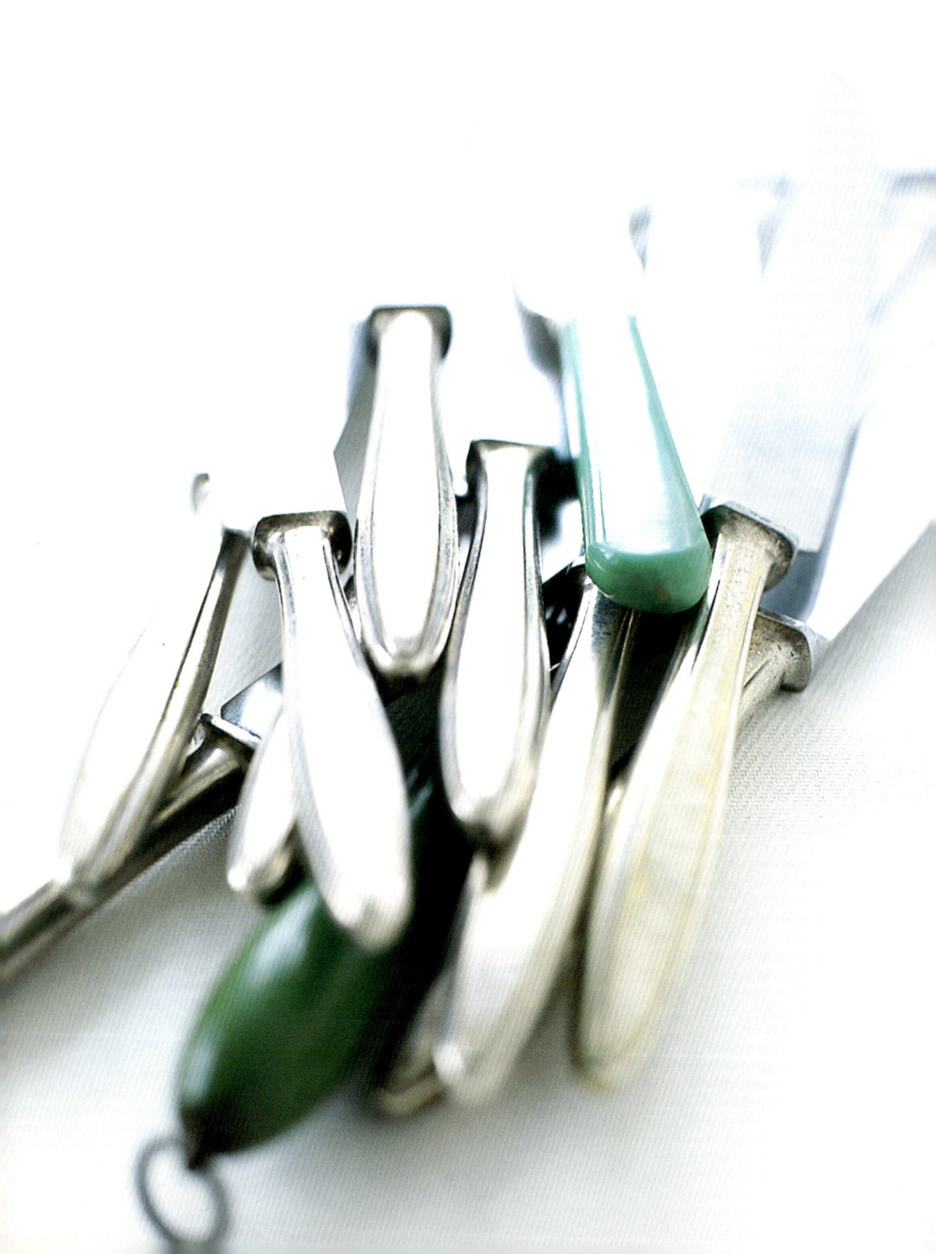

summer style

Bring your own summer style to the table. Juxtapose the everyday with the unusual, the old with the new. Mix and match—colours, china, glasses, napkins, cutlery. Use your eclectic collection of beautiful glasses for wine or water. Put those old bottles sitting at the back of the cupboard into action: fill them with summer blooms and glossy leaves, or group them together, empty, in the middle of the table as a quirky centrepiece. The cutlery you've inherited from your great-grandmother may take on a new lease of life when mixed with the shining silver set you were given for your twenty-first birthday. Find the beautiful little dessert forks you picked up at a garage sale and use them when serving cake at the end of a meal. A mismatched collection of open-necked glass containers can double as candle holders—the glass surrounding the candle will help keep any breeze from extinguishing the flame. A little bit of time and effort will pay off handsomely. Unusual centrepieces become talking points. Old china in muted tones brings a sense of history to the table. Don't be afraid to play with colour: soft blues and greens mixed with cream and white sing hot summer days; vibrant red, pinks and oranges fan the flames even more. Or you could cool your setting down with all white. From linen tablecloth to china to bowls and flowers, keep it pale and interesting.

Mix and match the old with the new

hurricane lamp

Make a hurricane lamp from an old jam jar. Twist a piece of wire around the opening to make a handle, then fill the jar with coarse sand to keep it stable. Place a candle inside and surround the lamp with seashells.

fresh fabrics

Instead of searching for a perfect tablecloth in the right shade, buy lengths of fabrics in wonderful summer colours and hem around the edges. Or use pinking shears for interesting detail and to prevent fraying.

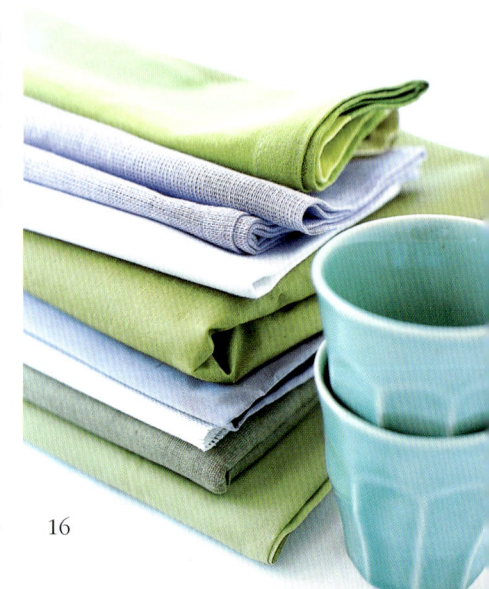

cream tea

Mix creams and white together for a fresh, simple effect. Use beautiful napkins or placemats to add accents of colour. Or for a truly stunning look, leave it all white, from china right down to the flowers.

eclectic hold-alls

Old green bottles and vintage cocktail glasses make great alternative vases for summer roses picked straight from the garden. Group them together in the middle of the table, or place on a nearby side table.

fresh flowers

Flowers, plants and greenery of all shapes and forms lend themselves to summer tables. Big bunches of deep-blue hydrangeas, small, hastily arranged full-bloom garden roses, bold groupings of fragrant lilies and small containers of dark-green succulents all make wonderful centrepieces. They inject colour, texture and a feeling of freshness to any setting. Unusual containers— old glasses, small tin buckets, china teapots, antique jugs, coloured bottles—are perfect for displaying flowers in all their fragrant glory. Blooms will last longer when stems are cut diagonally to ensure that the flowers absorb as much moisture as possible. Changing the water daily and cutting stems will also help.

Potted flowering plants take on a new lease of life when used on a summer table. Use small pots of daisies, geraniums or violets. They can be repotted into attractive terracotta or ceramic containers, but make sure the new container has proper drainage and enough space for the root structure. If flowers are too expensive or hard to get, try one of the many varieties of succulents. Succulents are easy to grow and stunning when grouped together. Many succulents are ready to be repotted in summer, so for a long-lasting and inexpensive table arrangement, unearth them from their regular pots and place in small ramekins filled with water. When ready, repot the succulent into a larger pot and place in a sun-filled location.

Succulents make great summer centrepieces

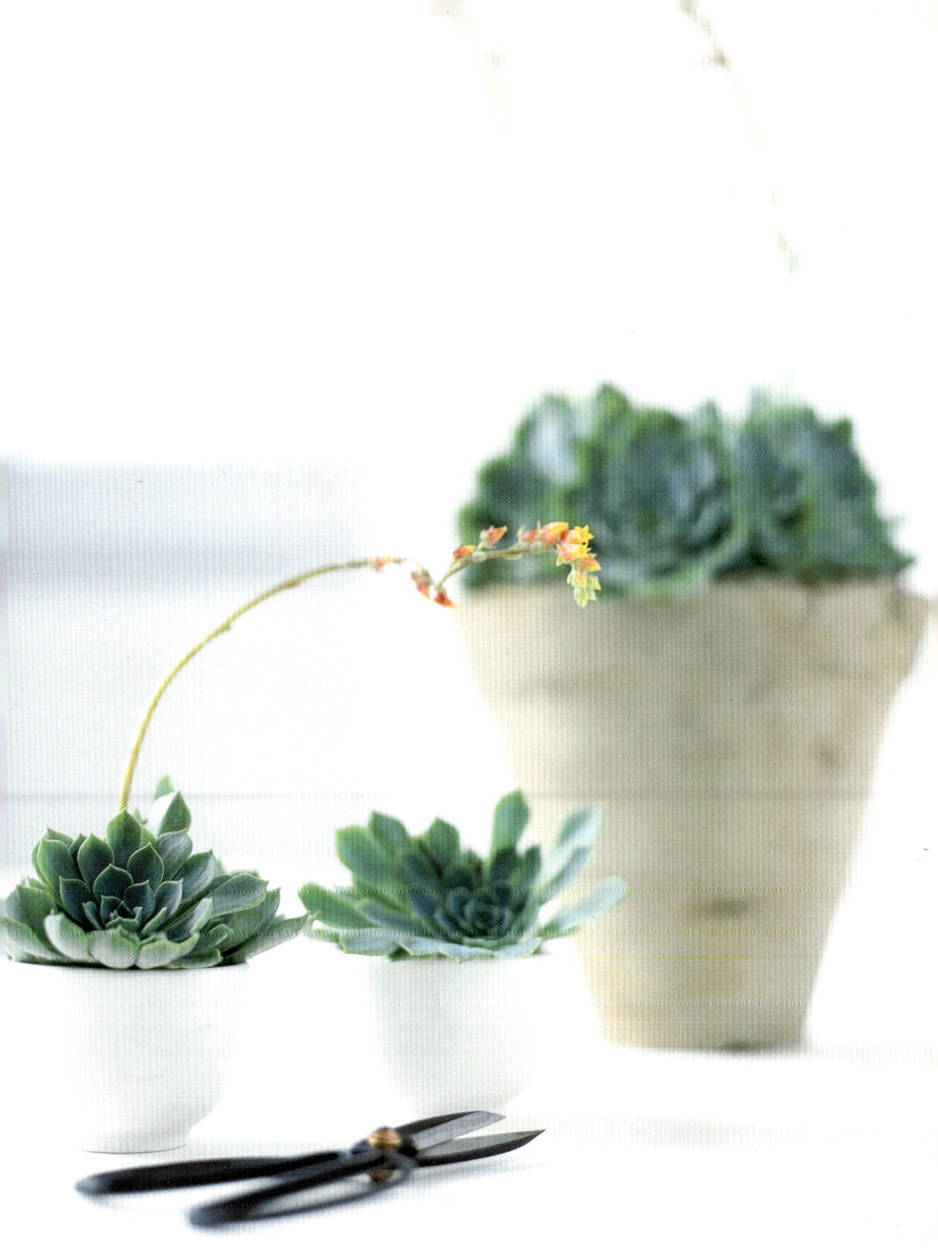

beach baubles

Seashells can make a wonderfully simple centrepiece. Run them along the length of the table or group them with candles. Try filling a pretty glass or jar with handfuls of interesting shells for a truly summer touch.

summer flowers

Hydrangeas are long-lasting summer flowers. They come in a range of colours, from deep blue to pink and white. To keep the flowers fresh, cut the stems and replace the water in which they stand every few days.

collectables

Collecting lovely old pieces like these vintage spoons takes time. Markets, antique auctions and garage sales are wonderful for uncovering unusual finds. Buy items when you come across them and store away for later use.

thirst quencher

Home-made cordial will quench even the biggest thirst. Make syrup from grated ginger, lemon zest, lemon juice and sugar. Heat gently in a saucepan and stir until the sugar is dissolved. Serve with ice, soda water and mint

summer

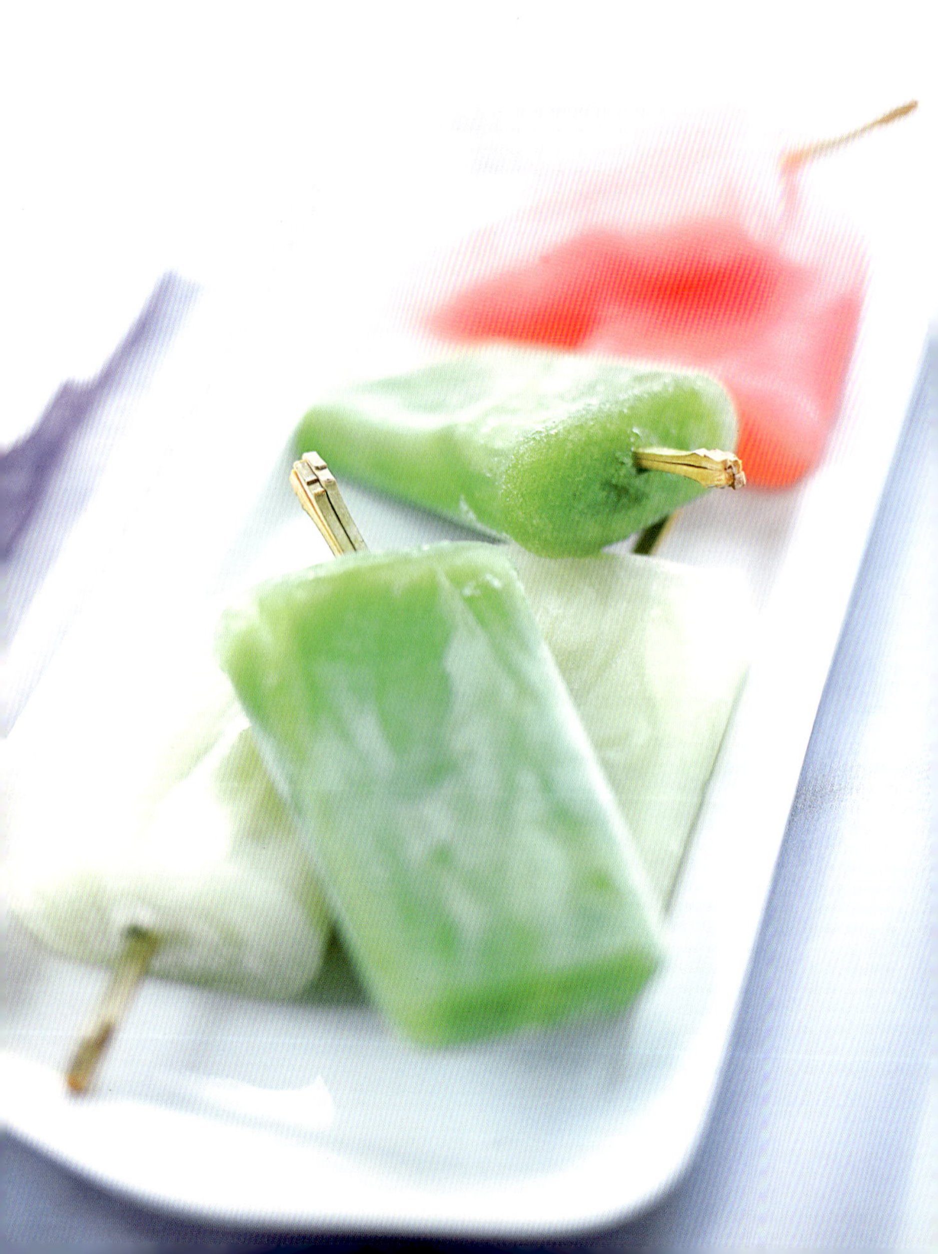

cool ideas

Cool colours and cool food are the pillars of a good summer table. When the heat is turned up, keep tones muted and refreshing. Icy blues and greens, cool pinks, pale cream and white all keep temperatures from rising. Use pale-coloured table linen mixed with white china. Big bowls of fresh flowers and fruit are a definite. Add cool elements to your table — jugs of iced water spiked with lime juice and mint leaves, carafes brimful of sparkling water laden with lemon and orange slices, home-made lemonade served in big glass pitchers or old-fashioned glass milk bottles, chilled water, wine and beer glasses (put in the fridge the night before and bring to the table at the last moment).

Turn large, colourful bowls into temporary ice chillers for wine or other bottles of drink. Buy or make quantities of crushed ice and pour around the bottles. Not only will you keep drinks cold, you'll also keep the table looking cool and welcoming. Freeze small fruit like strawberries and grapes for a delicious, cool mouthful. To complete the perfect summer meal, serve up your own blend of ice cream or sorbet, or for something different and tasty, try home-made icy poles. Make up your own concoction from summer-fresh fruit and juices. Our favourites are honeydew and mint, grape and lime juice, and ruby grapefruit juice. Icy pole moulds are sold in most good kitchenware stores.

Make your own mouthwatering icy poles

summer party

Summer is the ideal time to throw a party. Take advantage of the good weather and set up tables under blue skies or deep-velvet nights. Everything should be easy, relaxing and fun. Cover tables with a generous, heavy cloth and add flowers and candles. Throw handfuls of small blooms, like fragrant frangipani, randomly over the table linen for a pure summer feel—and a pure summer scent. Place small stacks of plates together with napkins and cutlery so everything is close by and easy to access. To keep things streamlined and simple, group cutlery in hold-alls: use old wooden cutlery trays, tall ceramic bowls or attractive metal containers to keep it all in one place. Try platters and bowls of varying heights to create different levels and give more interest to the table. Pile a pedestal cake plate with berries, have big bowls of mangoes and stone fruits, use an old ham stand for cold cuts, or use a layered cake stand for displaying different desserts.

Seamlessly blend the perfect lighting into your table equation. Give harsh lighting a wide berth and opt for something subtle. The delicate flicker of candlelight evokes romance and creates an old-fashioned elegance. Line the pathway to your table with waxed paper candle bags partially filled with sand (to stabilise them) and tea-light candles. Hurricane lamps are practical as well as attractive—all the romance of a candle, but with the flame kept safe from the wind. For a more celebratory atmosphere, search for colourful paper lanterns to place strategically around your table. Lengths of fairy lights threaded through trees and along fences also impart a festive feel. Tall bamboo torches add a tropical touch to any garden or courtyard. Fill with special lamp oil and the flame will be long-lasting; use torch oil with citronella and keep mosquitoes at bay. Remember to always place candles on fireproof surfaces, and don't leave any burning flame unattended.

Fragrant, fresh frangipanis are a wonderful addition to any summer table

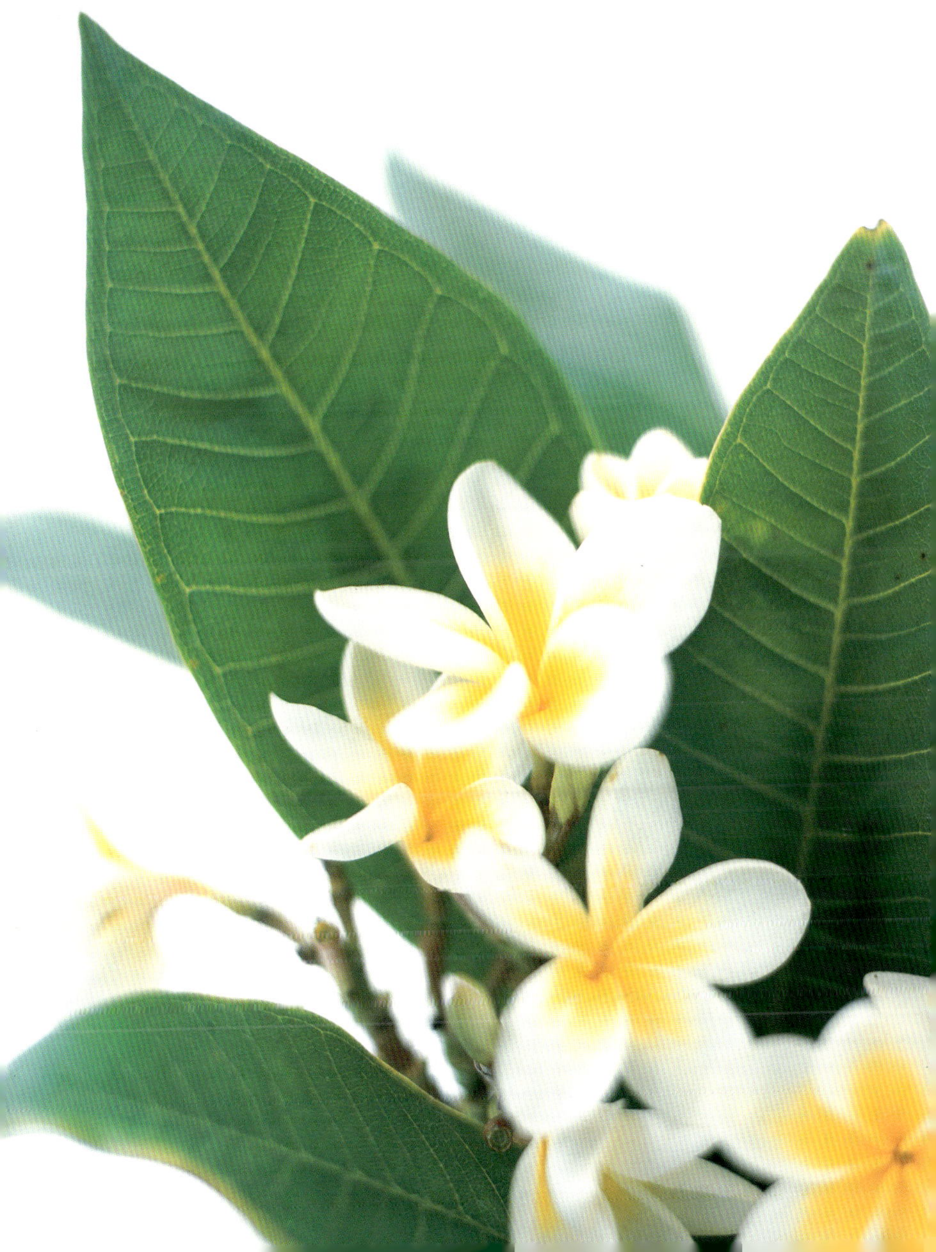

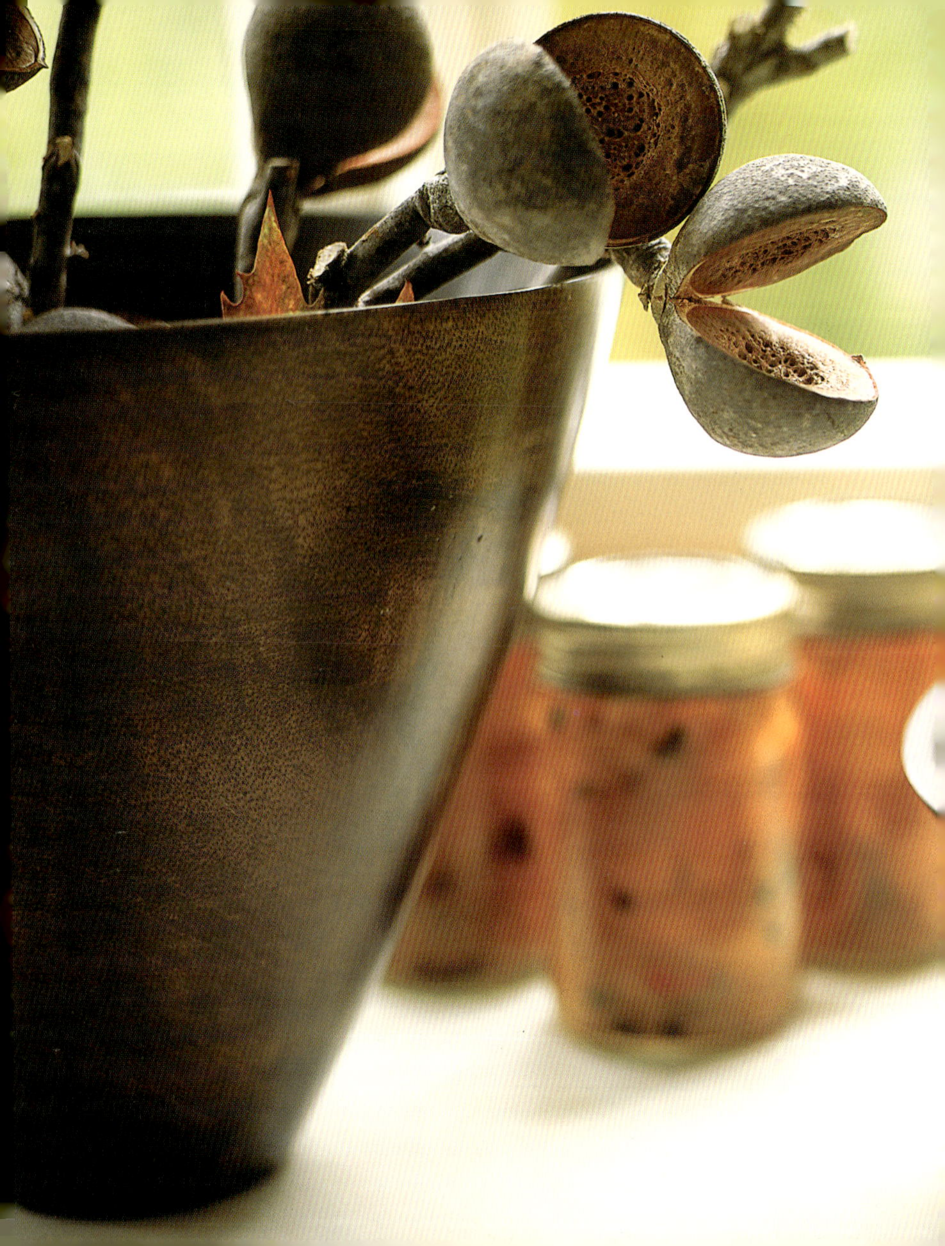

autumn

autumn colours

Just as you have a different set of clothes for summer, autumn, winter and spring, so should your table reflect the changes in the seasons. As the sun loses some of its intensity, colours go deeper and darker: russet, amber, ochre, gold and brown all give off a burnished glow. There is a definite chill in the air, and most dining goes back indoors. Tables become warmer and more intimate, but not necessarily contrived and busy. They can be sleek, modern and elegant—tables that are welcoming, tables that make you want to sit and linger over a meal. Let the food inspire you in your choice of table setting, and plan to make every meal memorable. From a cosy Sunday-night supper to an Asian banquet for ten, give your imagination free reign.

Carry your food theme through to your table. For an Asian-influenced meal, serve it on a low table in the living room. Use large, colourful floor cushions for seating, and team beautiful ceramic bowls with bamboo placemats and lacquered chopsticks. Scour markets for inexpensive and authentic pieces that will add character to your table, whether it is the dining table, coffee table or sofa table. Make every table work. Bring side tables into action, make a feature of a stunning coffee table, or enlist baskets, suitcases, old tea chests or antique blanket boxes for extra tabletop space. Keep decoration simple and ensure that your lighting is low and subdued. The glow of a single candle as a centrepiece is sometimes all that is needed to illuminate a table.

Theme your dinner, from the food to the table setting

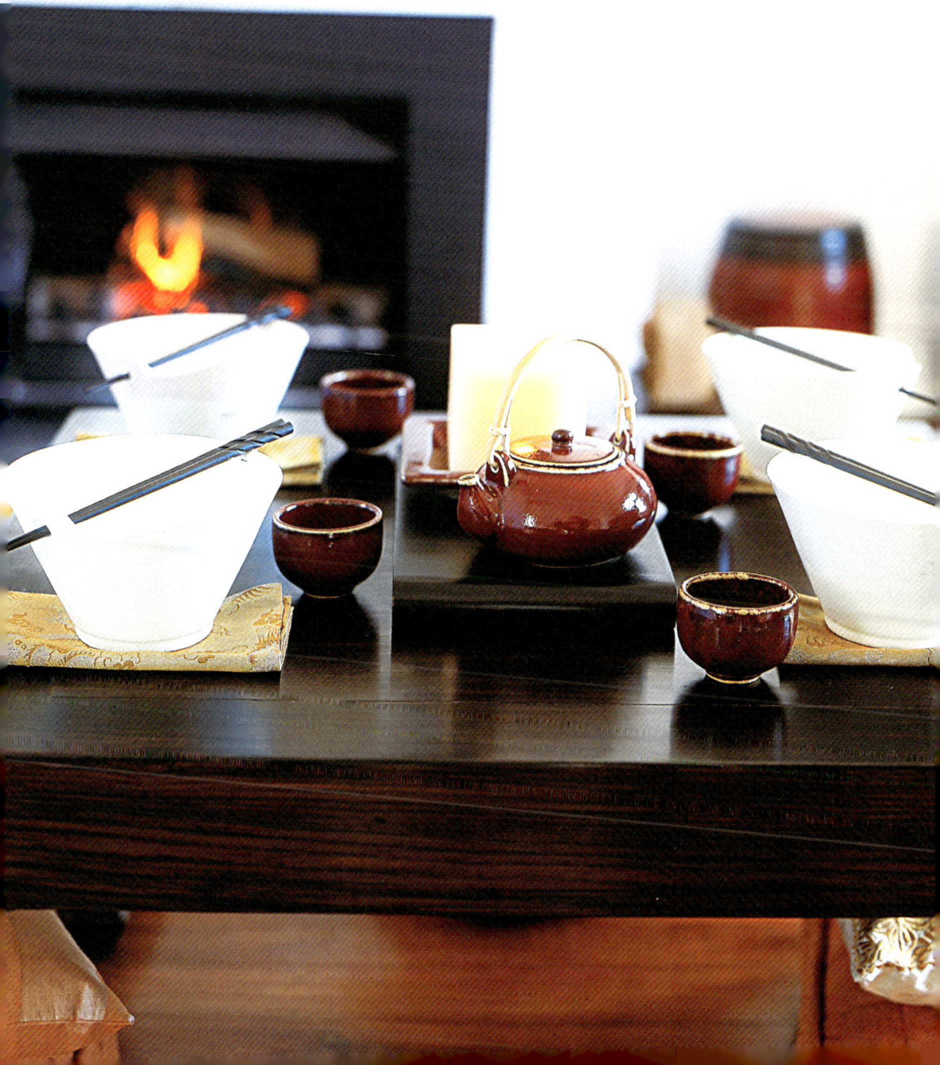

collectables
Side tables are great stages for showing off collectables. Here, an old glass ashtray looks perfectly comfortable in its starring role.

substitutions
Antique leather suitcases can be used as stunning-looking—and practical—substitutes for a traditional coffee table. They also double as storage space.

tea time

Serve tea in a beautiful teapot. Choose one that complements the mood of your table, be it romantic, modern, classical or traditional.

fragrant touches

Collect some autumn leaves and team them with fragrant pine cones for a long-lasting and sweet-smelling table decoration.

autumn

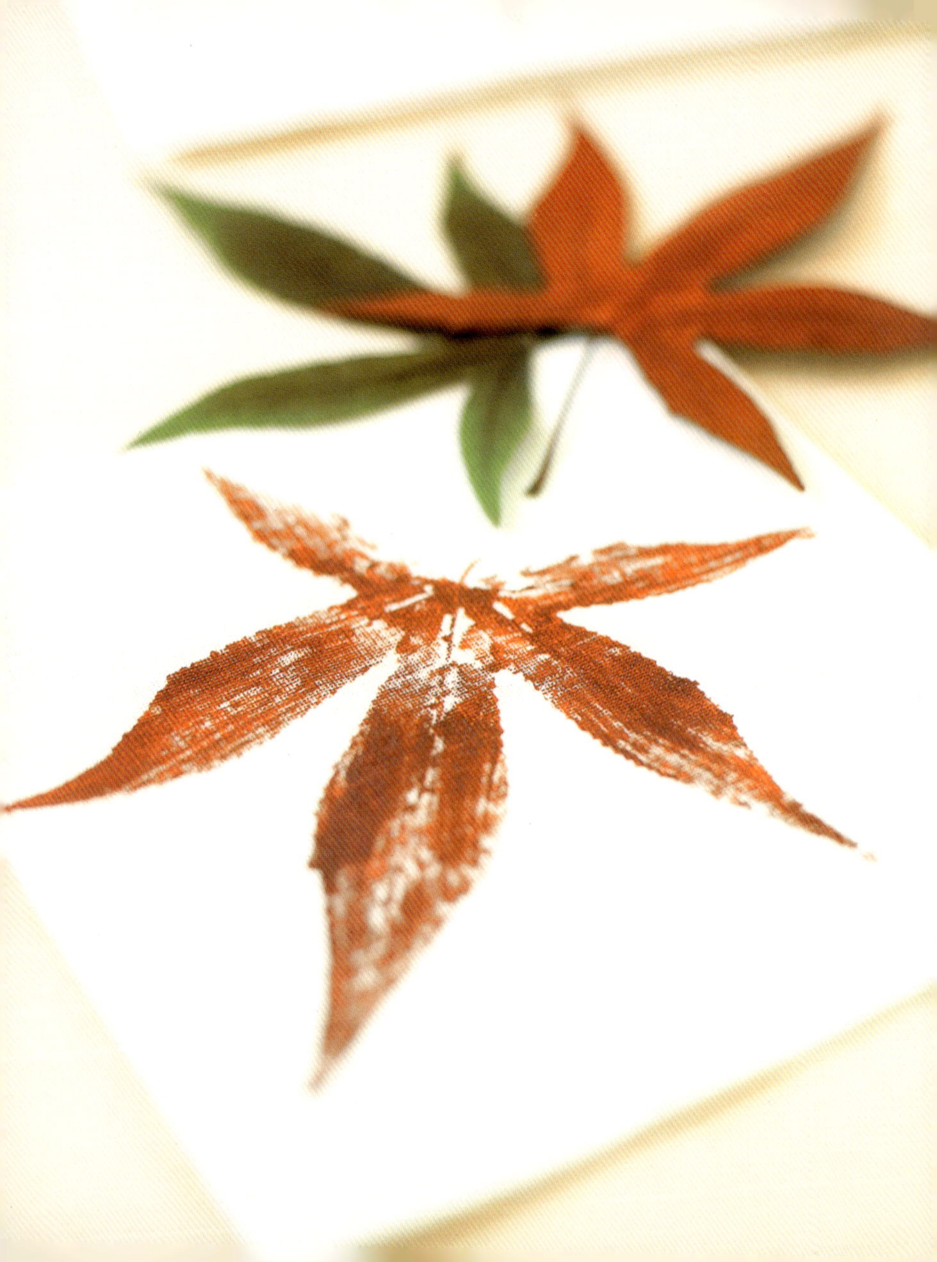

autumn beauty

Autumn has a beauty that's all its own: soft dappled sunlight, the bare limbs of trees, the ground covered in pine cones and the mesmerising shades of fallen leaves. It's not difficult to harness some of that beauty and incorporate it into your table so it reflects the season. Make a feature of the food you serve. Big platters of delicious roasted pumpkin, potatoes and turnips are a mouthwatering addition. Choose table linen in gorgeous autumn patterns and shades: oranges, deep greens, khakis, browns. Search for lengths of unusual fabrics and turn them into original tablecloths and napkins. Unleash your creative side: make your own napkins from attractive yet hard-wearing cloth, and embellish them by embroidering a small leaf or flower in one corner.

Try making your own placemats by painting an abstract pattern with watercolours on heavy paper and having the paper laminated. This will make the placemats hard-wearing and easy to clean. Unique touches bring a sense of character to any table. Personalise your napery by using simple methods like leaf printing. Buy fabric paints in autumn colours and some inexpensive, neutral-coloured napkins. Collect a few interesting flat leaves and, once dry, brush paint sparingly onto the leaf, press onto the napkin firmly, then remove carefully and leave the cloth to dry. Experiment with fabric painting. As you get more comfortable with the process, you might find yourself ready to take on bigger projects, like whole tablecloths,

A simple leaf print adds interest to plain napkins

autumn white
Simple white settings can work just as well in autumn as summer. Fill generous bowls with warming soups.

fabric touches
If you can't find table linen in the colours and patterns you desire, buy beautiful fabrics and make them into one-of-a-kind napkins, placemats and tablecloths.

autumn touches
Dried pods, leaves, unusual pieces of bark and driftwood all make eye-catching table decorations.

taste of autumn
Autumn is a great time to put a roast dinner on the menu. Arrange vegetables, like this delicious roast pumpkin, on big platters, and let the food take centre stage.

on the side

Keep in mind the other tables in your house and let them also change with the seasons. When flowers aren't in abundant supply, look for alternatives. Surround the base of candles with wheat grass or leaves for a simple yet stunning decoration. Fill a polished wooden bowl with things you've collected on long afternoon walks — pods, seeds and pine cones all are in generous supply throughout the cooler months, and they're free. When they lose their fresh, natural scent, perfume them with a few drops of your favourite essential oils. Mounds of berries, figs or plums look amazing piled high in a striking lacquered bowl. Fill big ceramic bowls with deep orange-coloured baby pumpkins or fresh green pears.

Collect some unusual handmade bowls and group them together; the simplest objects can take on a dramatic turn when used collectively. Round up some old bottles and fill them with small twigs or branches from fruit trees. Or go the photographic route: gather together old and not-so-old photographs, collect some beautiful frames and cover the tabletop with memories. If minimalism is more your style, pare it all down for striking effect. Sit a lone bowl on a sleek side table. Place one single spectacular bloom in a narrow-necked vase. Tulips, hyacinths and rosehips are all in season during autumn. Be bold, whether with an object of interest, something quirky or colourful, or a group of things you love.

Fill a beautiful bowl with dried wood nuts for a stunning focal point

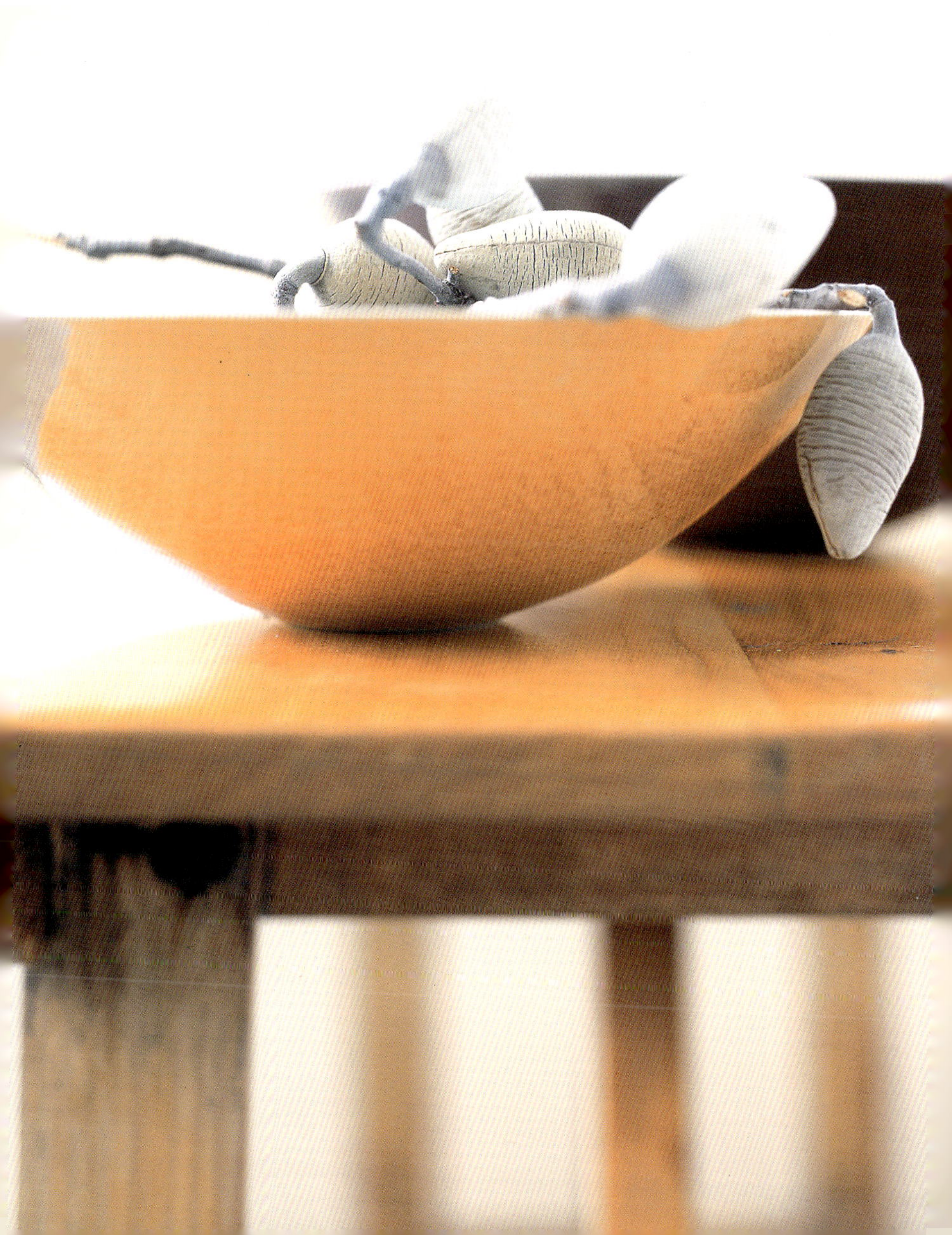

personalise it

For a truly unique touch, personalise your table linen. Try simple things, like adding a small cross-stitch pattern to a beautiful napkin.

fresh bread

There's nothing quite like the aroma of freshly baked bread. Knead and bake a few loaves from scratch, or try one of the many bread mixes now available from supermarkets.

wooden pegs

Try something different—like using wooden pegs as name tags. Paint on the names of your guests, let dry and attach to autumn-toned napkins.

combine colour

Deeper colours add warmth to a table. Combine colour with unusual touches: this orange Bakelite serving dish is complemented by the fresh green tones of a handful of miniature pears.

autumn

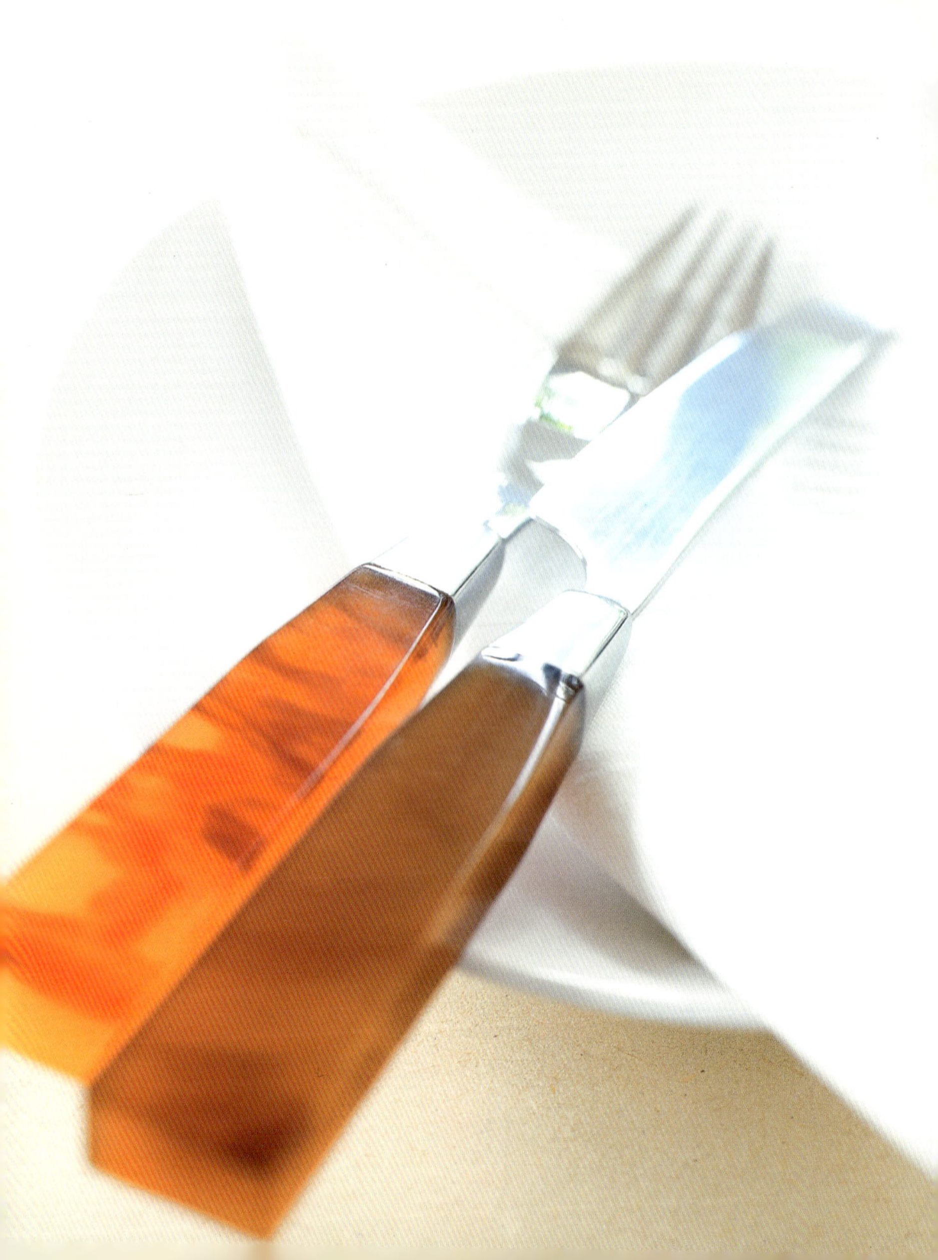

unusual touches

Don't always go for the traditional when it comes to decorating your table; blend the expected with the unexpected. Buy unusual pieces when you see them and add them to your collection. Uncover an old set of tiny ceramic pots and use them to hold pepper and salt. Buy tarnished but unusually shaped silver cutlery, polish it up and use it every day. Interesting oddities will add a touch of whimsy to the table. Elements don't have to be uniform, either. It's not the design of your table but the detail that will make it special. Give each setting its own personality—try placing a different but complementary napkin beside each plate (for example, use autumnal colours but different patterns, or try it the other way around—keep the patterns the same but use different autumn tones). Sit an autumn leaf beside the knife, on a napkin or underneath the stem of a glass. Home-made name cards or place-mats can add colour and a sense of structure to the table. Try using watercolours to paint simple images on thick paper, adding guests' names or initials and using them as place cards. Paint names onto unusual objects like large seed pods or leaves. If the table has a rustic feel, let small jars of home-made preserves double as place cards. Write names on some good-quality card, cut them out and glue them to the glass. Your guests can take them home as a parting gift.

Add beautiful yet unusual touches to your table, as with this amber-handled cutlery

autumn

special occasions

The way a table is set can determine the atmosphere of the occasion. Dictate the mood of your next event by the items you select and the way in which you arrange them. Decorate your table with care and beauty. Don't be afraid to use the 'good' china, your grandmother's silver cutlery or the best glasses for everyday eating. Use napkins. Put flowers in a beautiful glass and sit it in the middle of the table. Throw on that lovely linen tablecloth, even if you're only eating by yourself. Give all meals a sense of occasion—a bowl of soup and some hot buttered toast take on a new lease of life when served in style.

Include elements that demand attention: tall ceramic bottles in muted shades of blue and green, a striking antique bowl, or glass decanters glowing with liquor. Fill an antique sugar bowl with mints or toffees. Make every table intimate and special. Keep lighting simple and subdued, and never underestimate the power of candlelight. Dot candles at random around your dining area, not just on the table. Use a mixture of candle holders—the good sterling silver ones along with the market-day finds. Group them together on a side table, in a line along a mantelpiece, on the sideboard. Candlelight alone has the power to make a meal feel special.

Tall glass decanters too beautiful to hide away

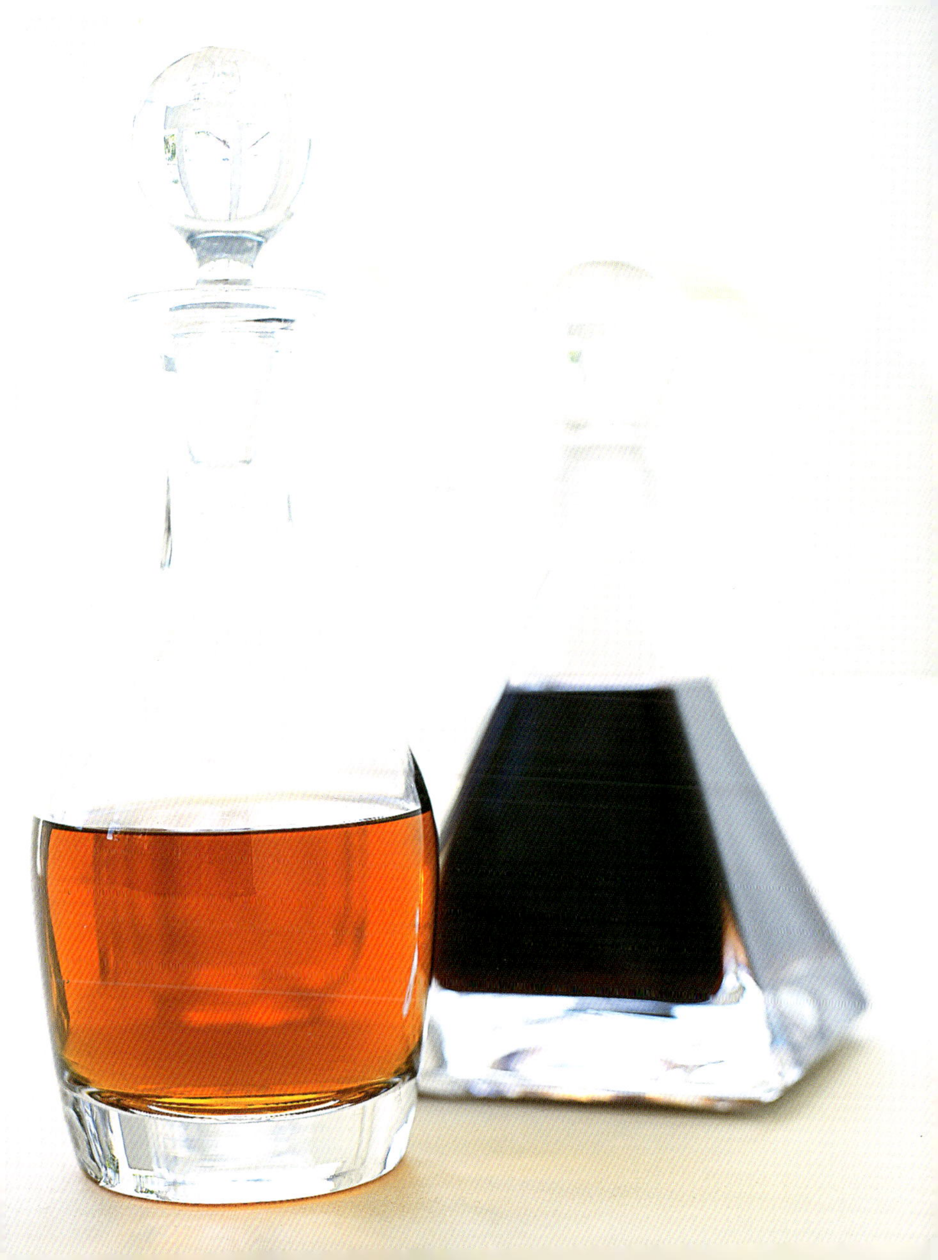

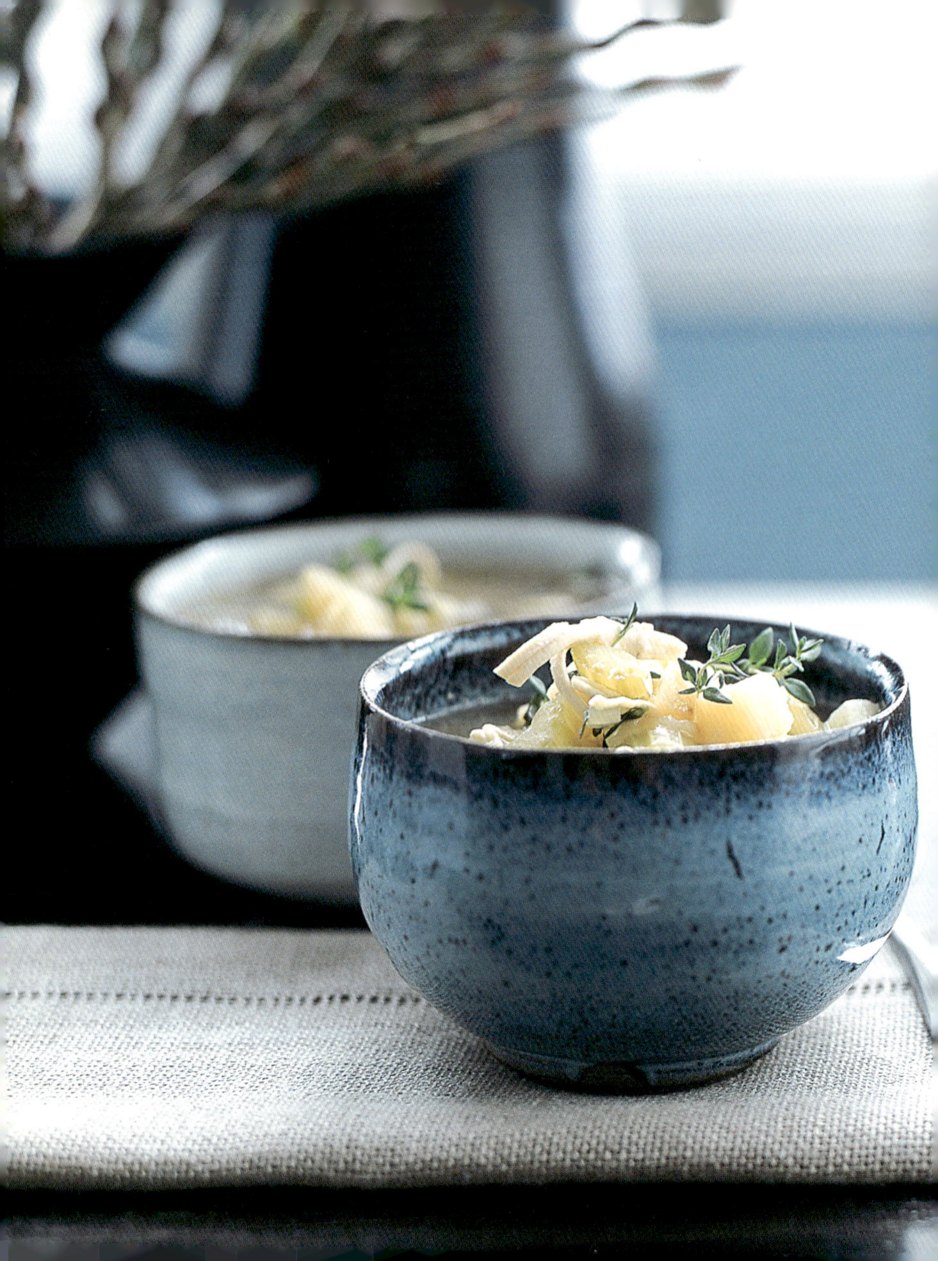

winter

dramatic times

In winter, go for drama: intense, passionate colours, a sophisticated edge. Darker colours lend warmth and intimacy to their surroundings and, in winter, this makes for a more inviting space in which to relax and enjoy good food and conversation. Rich reds, black, brown, burgundy and crimson are great winter-based colours. Try mixing them with lighter tones for a more contemporary feel. Make your table comfortable. Plan for plenty of elbow room so that guests feel at ease, not crowded. Allow the table an abundant elegance—big plates, deep bowls, large glasses, generous mugs and cups, masses of flowers. Make sure your dining area is warm and intimate; even if it's afternoon tea served in the kitchen, the room should be comfortable so that everyone feels relaxed. Lighting plays an important part in creating an intimate atmosphere, and what better way to create intimacy than with an open log fire. Fires do double duty by giving off a wonderful, flattering glow as well as keeping the room warm and snug. Candles are a must and can make a dramatic stand when used alone. Try an unusually large white candle placed alone on a simple white plate. For something more sumptuous, surround the base of the candle with small, full-bloom flowers and lots of soft green moss. Or try making your own candles. Candle-making kits are sold through most craft shops.

Mix dark winter shades with lighter colours for dramatic appeal

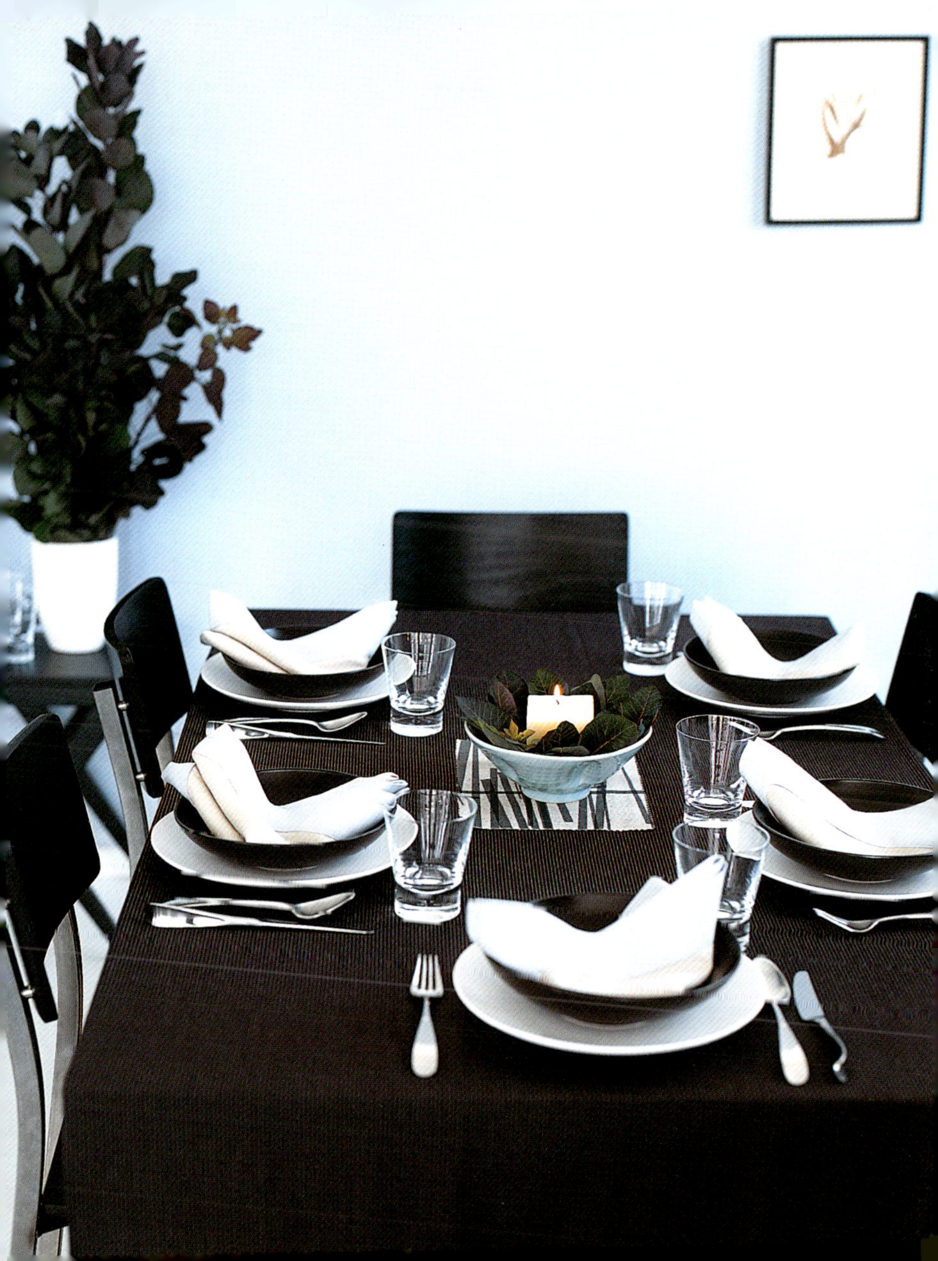

keep it simple

Keep food simple but tempting. Beautifully ripe brie with a bunch of dark grapes can be a perfect way to finish off a warm, winter meal.

special effects

Embed dried herbs such as star anise, cinnamon sticks, bay leaves, citronella leaves and cloves into hot wax to make your own fragrant candles. Wax and wicks are sold through craft shops.

dining easy

Hearty winter soups fill the stomach and soothe the soul. Serve in big, robust bowls with lots of warm bread for a quick, easy, intimate supper.

sixties style

Elegant sixties-design glassware is making a comeback. Rummage through second-hand shops, markets or retro furniture stores, and try to get hold of full sets for dramatic impact.

winter

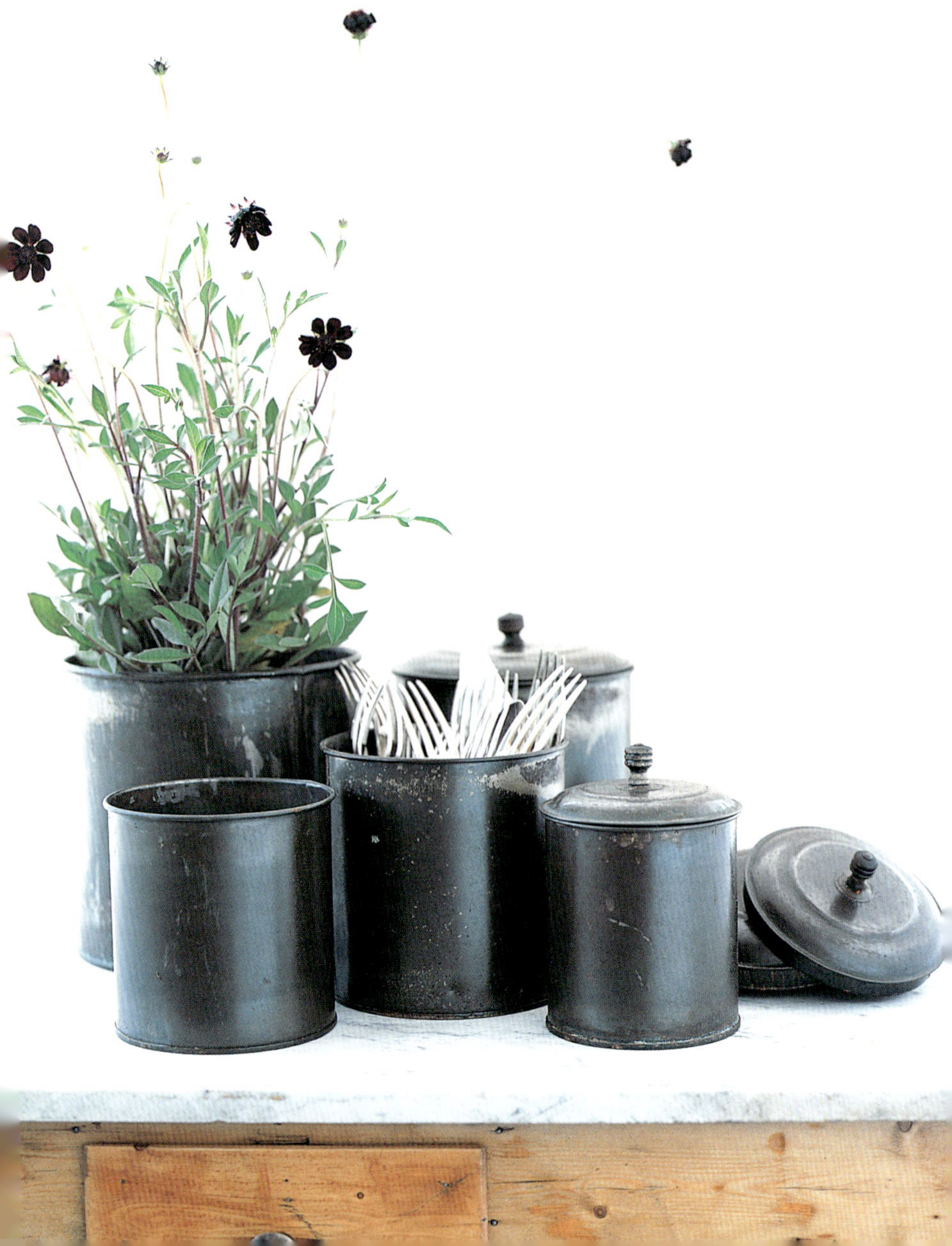

a place for everything

Some things are just too beautiful to hide away, so if they look good, leave them out on display. Tabletops don't have to be used only for eating; they can be enlisted to help with storage problems too. If you're pushed for space, be creative and make what space you do have—sideboards, shelves, side tables—work. Beautiful fabric placemats can be used as a highlight on a sleek side table. Others can be rolled up and stored in a wicker basket or left folded on a small tray or plate. Unusual bowls can be used to hold candles, toffees, keys or spare coins. Cutlery can be stored in wooden trays, a set of old metal canisters or in jars. Put an eclectic collection of pots, bottles or vases into action. Use some to hold flowers, others to hold incense, one to hold rolled-up napkins. Buy interesting lacquered or fabric-covered boxes and use them to hold receipts, bills and mail. If there is no room for a drinks cabinet, put glasses, bottles and decanters on display, but make sure everything is clean, polished and dust-free. Use a theme to tie everything together—colour, texture, shape or material. Then let the whole ensemble take on a life of its own.

A collection of old canisters looks great and helps with storage problems

monogrammed linen
Leave beautiful napkins on display. Fold and place a small stack flat on an attractive plate or platter, or roll up and stand in a bowl or basket.

must-have decoration
Place candles in a container so the wax doesn't drip onto the table. This square candle is surrounded by glossy winter leaves and set in a round ceramic bowl.

table

extra space
Use side tables as extra serving space. Pull a side table close to the main table, drape with a beautiful piece of fabric and set up as a drinks table.

mix and match
Mix and match different-coloured ceramics and glassware on your winter table, but remember to keep the overall look clean and simple.

winter

scent from heaven

Our sense of smell can be crucial to what we enjoy and how much we enjoy it. Scents evoke memories—warm, perfumed skin after a bubble bath, freshly cut grass on long walks in the country, the salty smell after a day at the beach, the warm and comforting aroma of freshly baked scones. Paying attention to the scent of a room is imperative, especially when entertaining. The room should have a pleasant but not powerful aroma, one that is sympathetic to the meal you are serving. It should be subtle enough to complement the food, not overpower it. Flowers are a perfect way to perfume a room, but make sure the scent is soft—fresh roses give off a beautiful, subtle fragrance that won't clash with food smells. For a more evocative aroma, choose an oil burner and opt for one of the many essential oils. Each oil has its own unique properties, so choose carefully and ask for some advice from an aromatherapy expert if you're not sure. Jasmine is perfect for a romantic dinner for two. Try some geranium oil to help create a relaxed atmosphere, or some clary sage oil, which is said to encourage lively conversation. Sometimes, though, the best aromas are those that come from the kitchen, especially in winter: the smell of freshly baked bread brought hot to the table, a warm apple pie left cooling on the windowsill, or a just-made batch of chocolate-chip cookies.

The aroma of a warm apple pie is a welcome winter's treat

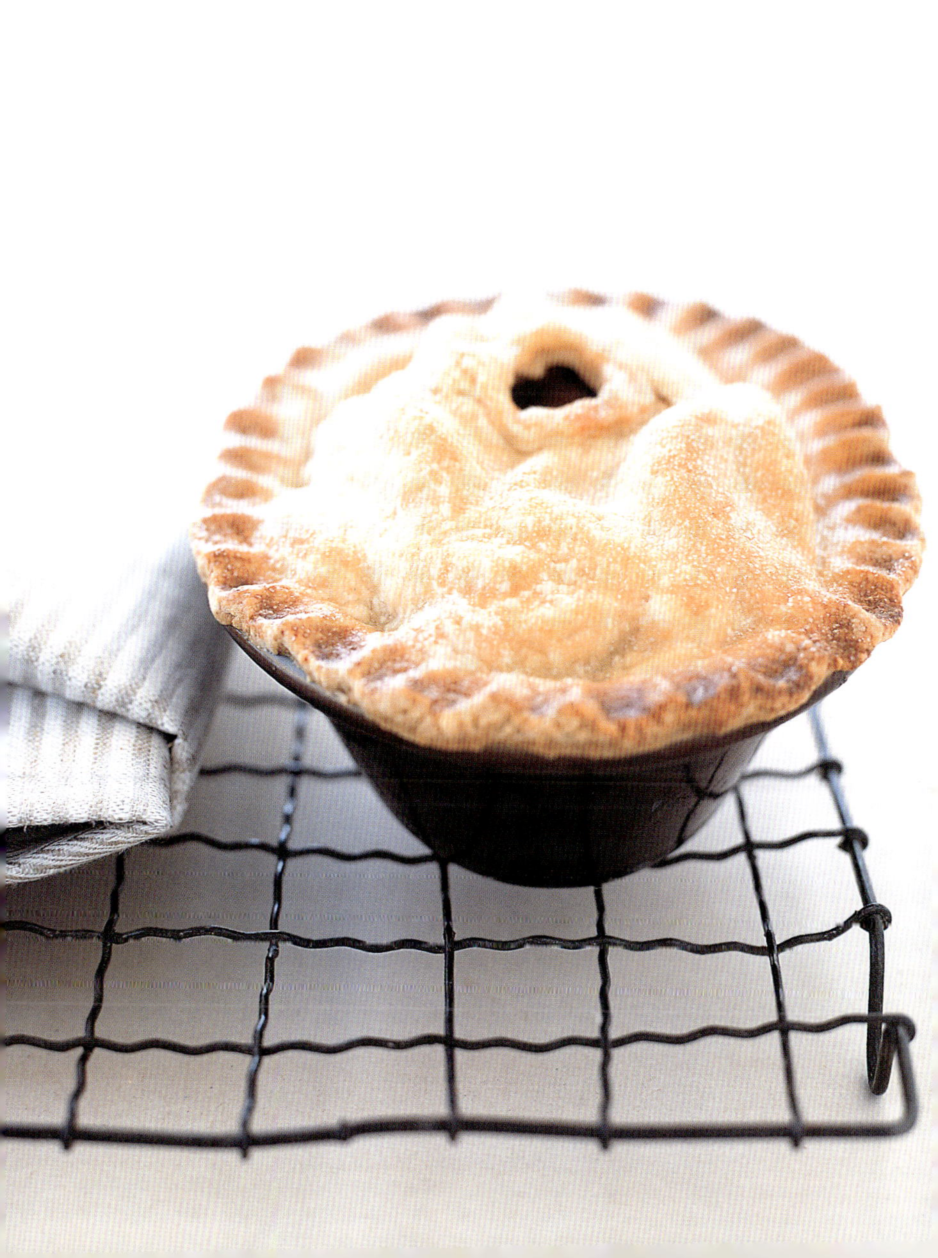

hard-wearing fabrics

Buy table coverings and napkins made from hard-wearing fabric such as hemp or linen. These fabrics have great textures, are easy to press and stay looking good for a long time.

new-age napkins

Old linen tea towels, cut into small squares and hemmed, make great cocktail napkins. Or cut them slightly bigger for dinner or cake napkins.

home-made invitations

Place a leaf between sheets of waxed paper, cover with a cloth and iron to bond the paper together. Stick the waxed paper to good-quality paper to complete an individual dinner invitation.

in detail

A beautiful table is all about attention to detail. Special touches, like these unusual salad servers, will help to make your table unique.

winter

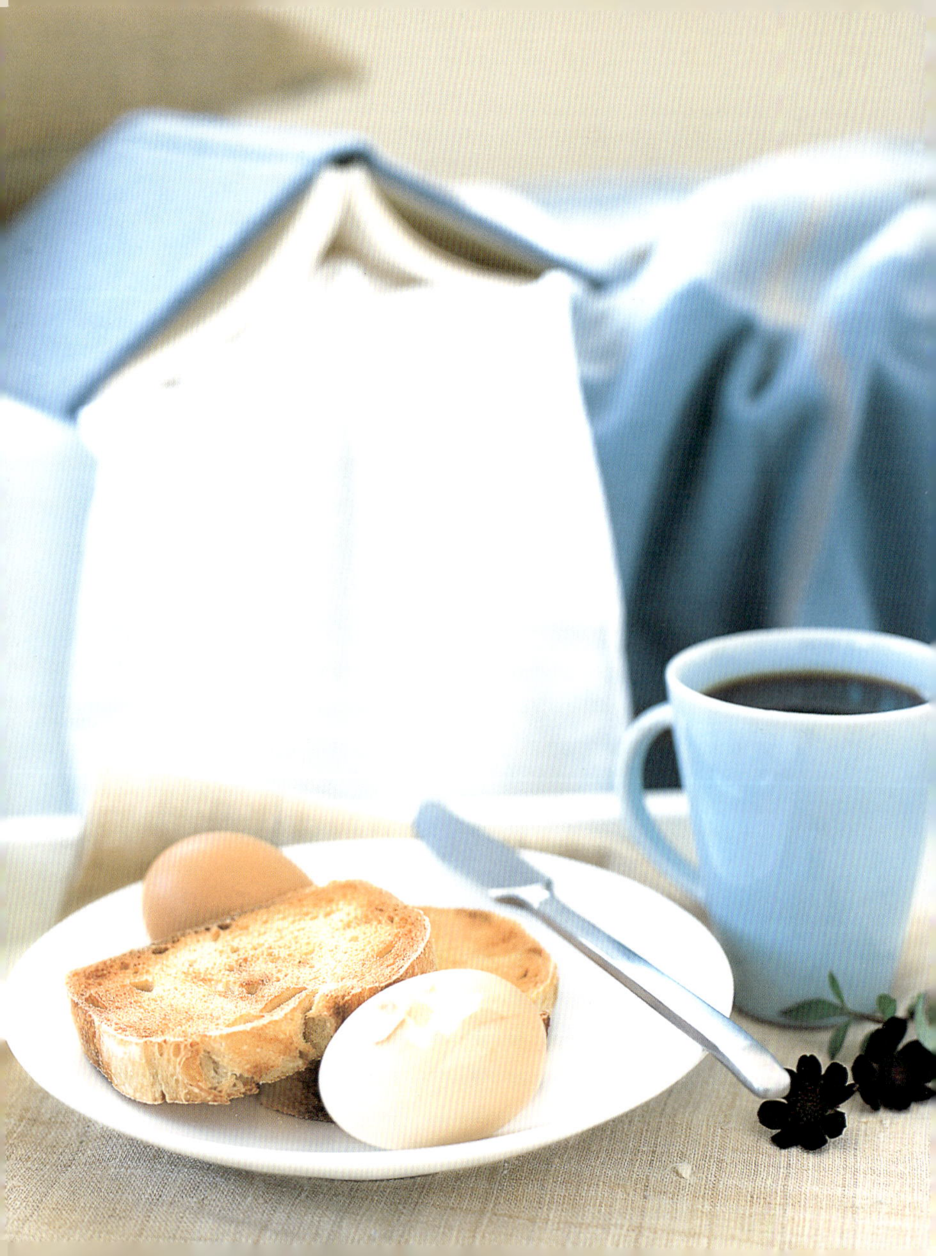

dining in style

There's nothing quite like breakfast in bed on a cold morning. Snuggled under sheets and blankets, with large, plump pillows propping you up, the world's worries can wait until later. Warm toast, hot tea, just-right eggs and the morning's newspaper complete the scene—a perfect way to start the day. Set a breakfast tray with just as much care as you would a table, whether it's for you or a loved one. A beautiful cloth, good china, gleaming cutlery and one or two small blooms can make the experience special. Let the tray reflect the occasion. For an everyday breakfast, keep it simple: don't overwhelm the tray with the opulent or the grandiose, and let the food take centre stage. For a special occasion, though, *do* go overboard. Cover the tray in fragrant petals, make a pot of real tea in your most beautiful teapot, add a small ceramic jug of milk or slices of lemon. If coffee's more your cup of tea, make a plunger of coffee and let the rich aroma fill the room. Instead of toast on a plate, use a small wicker basket lined with a cloth napkin and filled with warm croissants or toast. Put a pat of butter in a small ramekin and fill another pretty pot full of jam or honey. Maybe you've taken to your bed later in the day, with a tray groaning under the weight of a huge bowl of soup, toast and a glass of wine? The rules are the same. In fact, there's just one: make your tray as pleasing to the eye as it is to the stomach.

Keep breakfast in bed simple and relaxing

go for drama

A table setting has to accommodate many possible variations. Whether the occasion is formal or casual, whether the meal is for one person or a posse, whether it's a celebration or a quiet afternoon catch-up with friends, tables can take on any number of different personalities. The winter table is all about relaxation, warmth and comfort. This can be achieved through the choice of colours used for table linen, the colours and textures of plates and bowls, and the decorations used. Darker colours add warmth to their surroundings, evoking a feeling of comfort and relaxation. Add a lighter colour such as white, stone or cream for a fresh take on the traditional. Winter tables look great when pared down and streamlined. Let the colours add the drama, and keep clutter to a minimum. A simple setting of a plate, bowl, cutlery, napkin and a water or wine glass looks stunning laid out on a textured black cloth. Winter table decorations should stay in line with the effect you want to achieve. If stark and simple is what you're after, try a single lit candle surrounded by glossy green leaves. A small bowl of winter flowers or rich red berries will look great in the centre of a sparsely decorated table. Many flowers are expensive in winter, so be creative. Small pots of moss make a stunning focal point, as do a collection of variegated leaves. Keep it simple and stylish and your winter table will be a welcoming one.

A textured dark-brown cloth is a good foundation for any winter setting

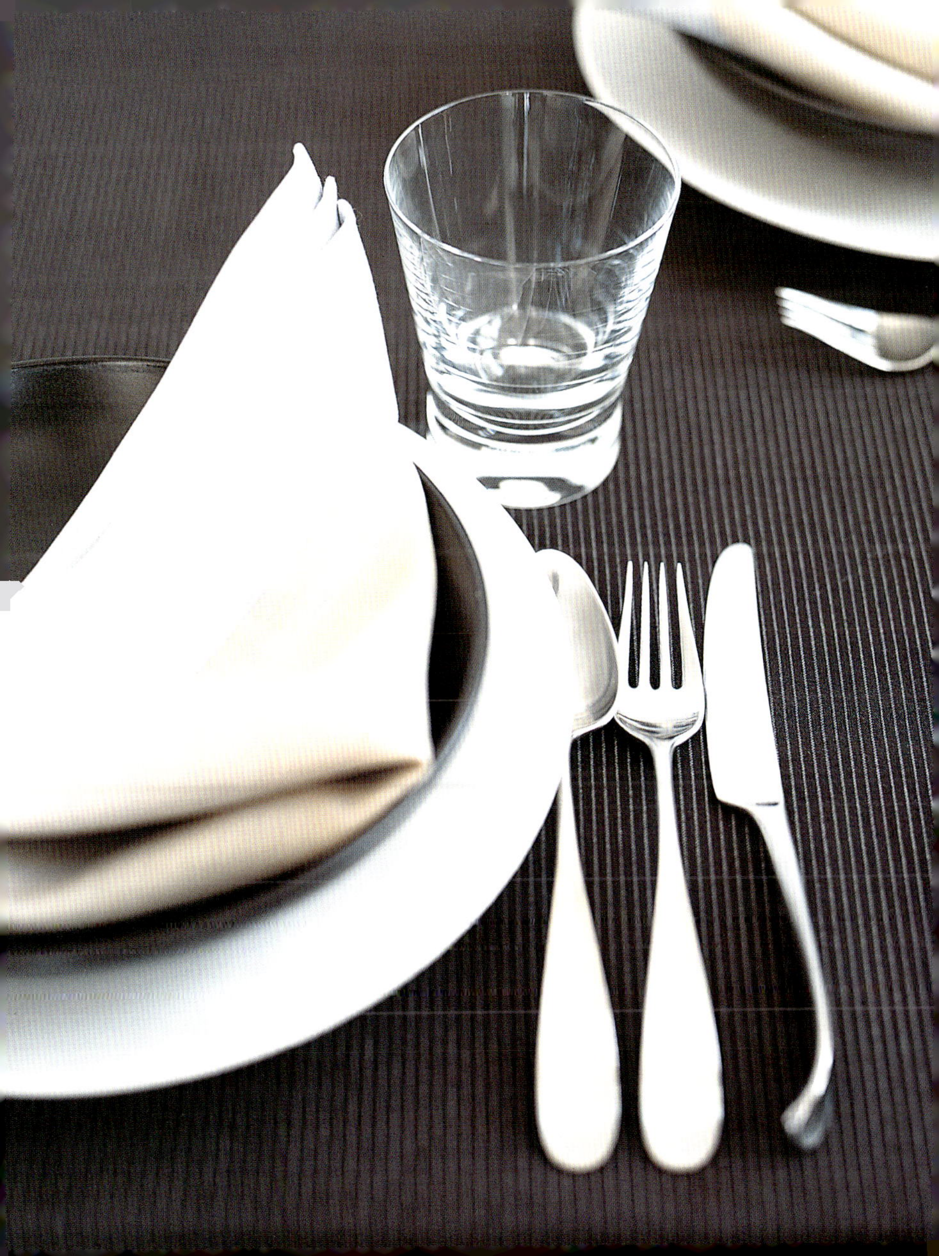

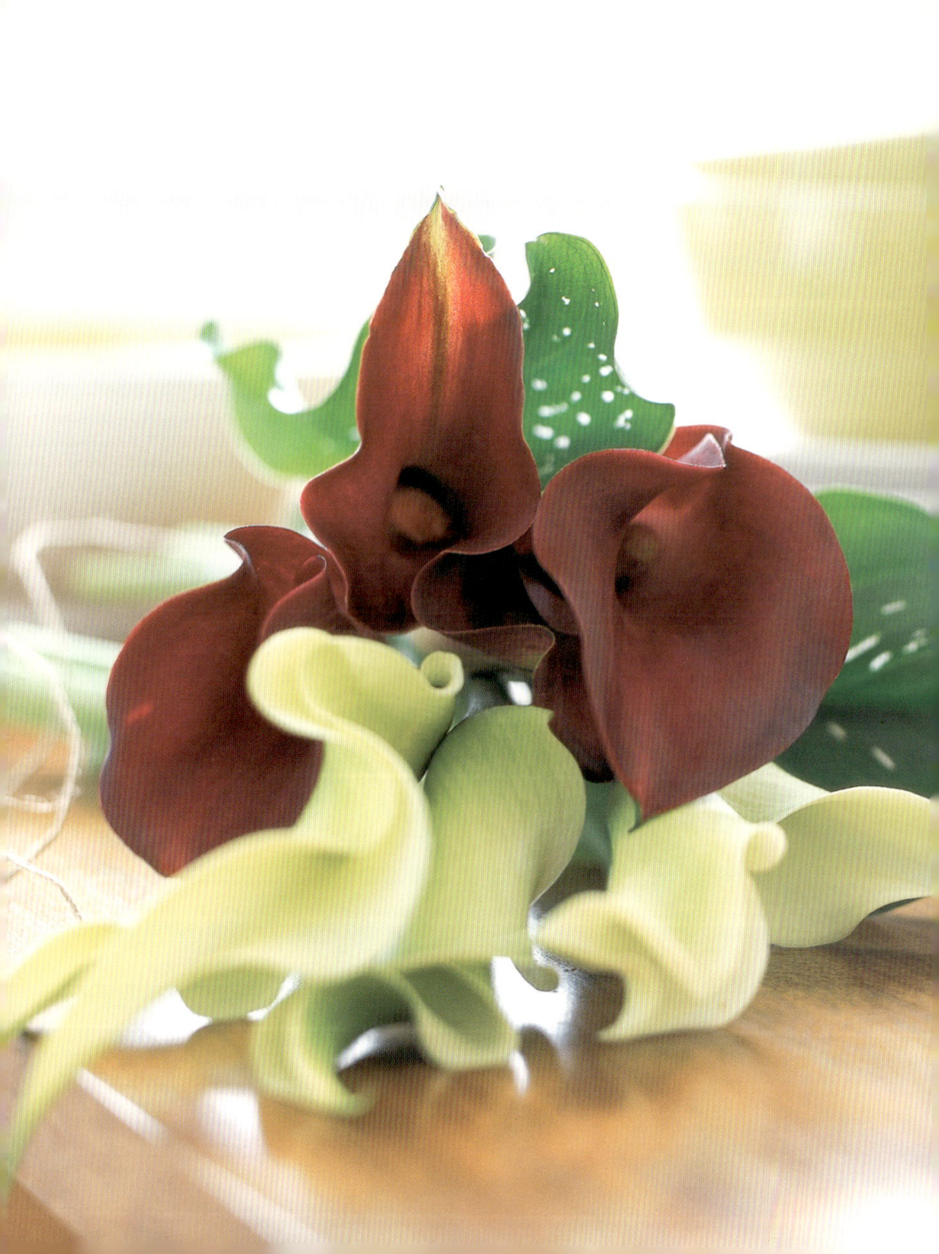

spring

fresh, pretty, light

Spring is all about romance. It's the season of new beginnings and all that accompanies them: fresh air, mild days, luscious fruit, sweet-smelling flowers. Spring moves people to celebrate. It's the time for memorable occasions, like weddings, engagements and parties. The colours of this season are mouth-watering—pale green, lavender, pink, white—and the look is delicate, light and pretty: beautiful, sheer cloths, simple glassware, flickering candles. Keep elements fresh, inspiring and romantic. Spring flowers like deep-purple hyacinths, fragrant freesias, sunny yellow daffodils, fresh jonquils and elegant tulips are all in abundance.

Put them in unpretentious glass vases or use a set of small, understated water glasses to set them off to best advantage. Place flowers everywhere. Pick a handful of full-blown roses from the garden to decorate the sideboard, and line the windowsills with pots of geraniums or tulips. Harness the soft natural daylight if you are planning a brunch or lunch—set your table up in a room with large windows so that sunlight will stream in, or take a table outdoors into the garden. At night, keep lighting soft with lamps and candles. Food should be in keeping with the atmosphere: light, pretty and appealing to the eye as well as to the palate.

Crisp, fresh colours and delicate touches lend a sense of occasion to this table

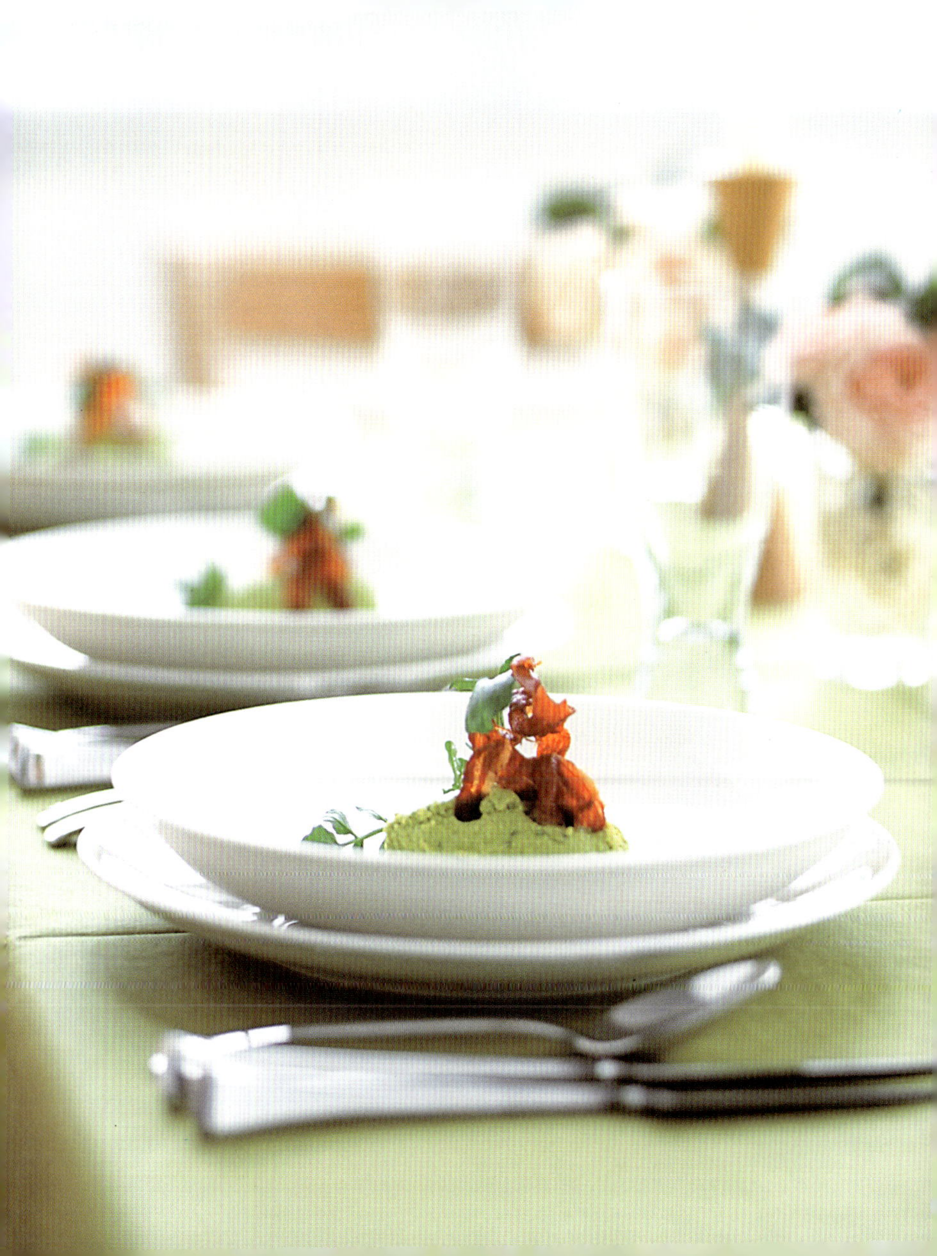

chic leaves

Add lovely touches to your spring table with items like these leaf plates and candle. Keep your eyes peeled for similar articles at local markets and in homeware stores.

appetising mouthful

Keep food light, simple and tempting. Broad-bean paste topped with crispy prosciutto takes on a spring feel when decorated with a sprig of watercress and a drizzle of extra-virgin olive oil.

fresh flowers

Nothing shouts spring like beautiful fresh flowers. A simple glass is the perfect container for these gorgeous pink roses. String has been wrapped around the stems for added interest.

budding bounty

Try something different on your brunch or lunch table. A small branch from a fruit tree that's laden with its budding bounty makes for a fresh and simple table decoration.

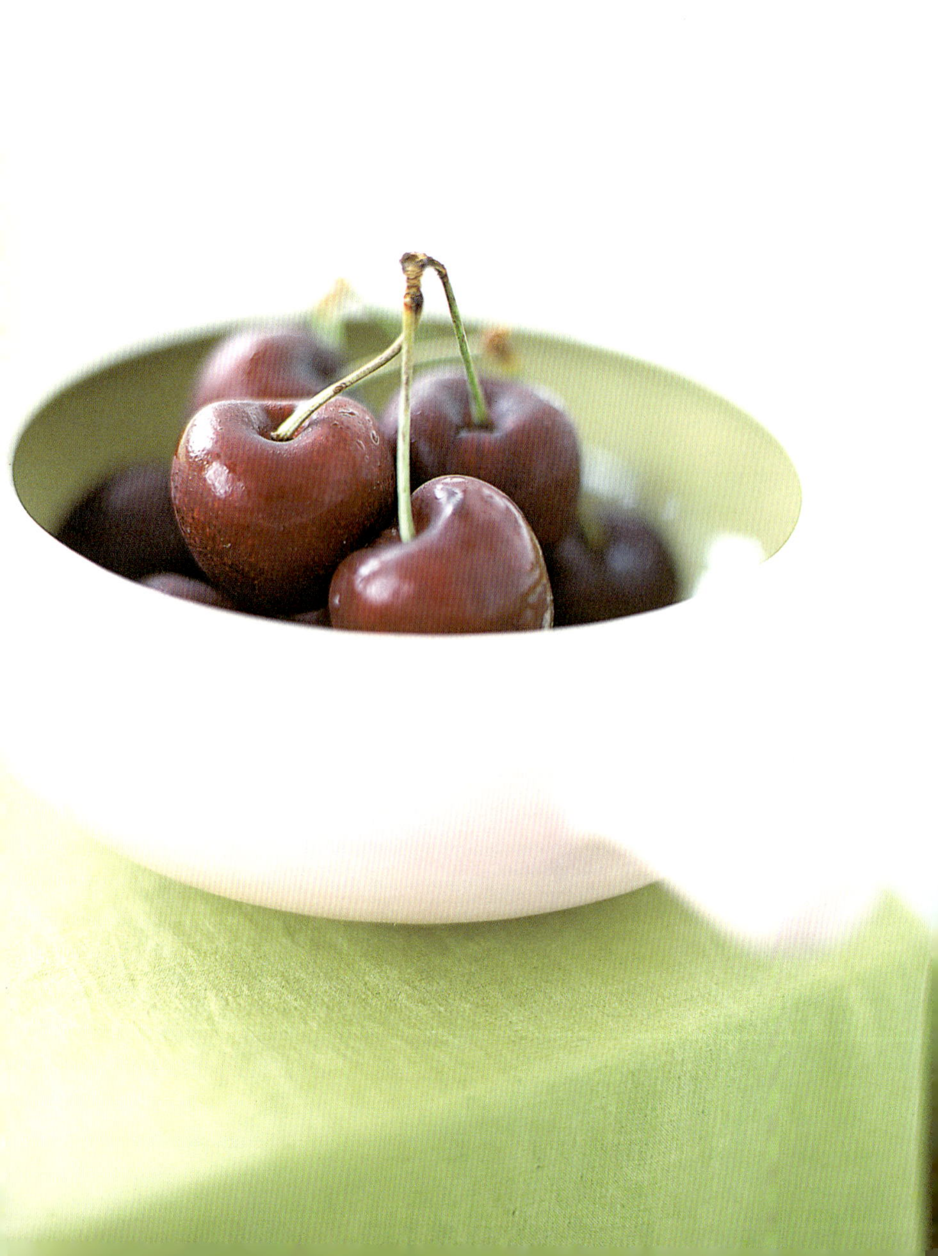

fruit flavoured

Flowers aren't the only way to go in spring. There is such an abundance of produce that flowers can be retired from time to time to let other spring essentials take their place. Cherries, grapes and berries are starting to make an appearance in the markets at this time of year and make eye-catching centrepieces. Pile high a small cake stand with a pyramid of strawberries and set it in the middle of a table in place of flowers. Fill a pretty hand-blown glass bowl full of luscious, rich-red cherries. Make delicious fruit-juice toffees, wrap them in cellophane and serve in a polished silver bowl. Mix the colours of the fruit with the rest of your table for a bright, pretty look.

Reflect the colours of the season in table linen. A strawberry-pink or soft-green fabric draped across the table immediately evokes the feel of spring. Complement your cloth with coloured fabric napkins, or use brilliant white or cream napkins for contrast. China can be simple or more embellished. This is the time to bring out beautiful pieces that you've been given or the treasures you've collected. Patterned or textured plates in pink, green and lavender will make lovely features. Use them as accents to white china or, if you have enough, make them the highlight of each place setting. Use the colours and fruits of spring to enhance your table and bring it to life.

Deep-red cherries piled high can make wonderful table decorations

spring

calla lilies

The vibrant colours of fresh calla lilies make a stunning centrepiece. Arrange casually in an unusual glass vase or a beautiful water jug for an eye-catching feature to a spring table.

unique china

Use collected pieces of china to give tables a unique feel. Mix different styles and patterns, using colour as a common theme.

spring table

Seek out fabrics in fresh, clean colours, such as this eye-catching green, and turn into simple, stylish tablecloths. Team with white china for a stunning spring look.

berry ripe

Ripe and unripe berries piled on a small ceramic plate look deliciously fresh. Home-made fruit toffees, wrapped in cellophane, are an additional treat.

spring

perfect picnic

The mere mention of spring evokes the image of a perfect picnic. The anticipation of fresh air, warm skies and good food whets the appetite and sends moods soaring. Picnic tables—whether they be an actual table or a rug thrown over lawn or sand—can be as pleasing to the eye as any other.

Cover a picnic table with a cloth in fresh spring colours, or spread a lovely big checked rug on the ground in preparation for what is to come. Toss in some big cushions or pillows for comfortable lounging. Take cutlery and cloth napkins. If you don't want to take china or glasses for fear that they will get broken, scout around for an attractive plastic picnic set. Try to find one in true spring colours, and merge both the practical and the aesthetic. Pretty plastic tumblers are available in great colours and are particularly appropriate when there are children along. If it's a grown-up picnic, throw caution to the wind and carefully pack china plates and glasses for a truly celebratory feel. Include a few beautiful bowls and pile them high with green salad leaves or grapes and berries. Food should be portable, simple yet delicious to add a fine finish to a wonderful open-air experience.

A selection of tiny treats wrapped in a paper cone and tied with ribbon grass

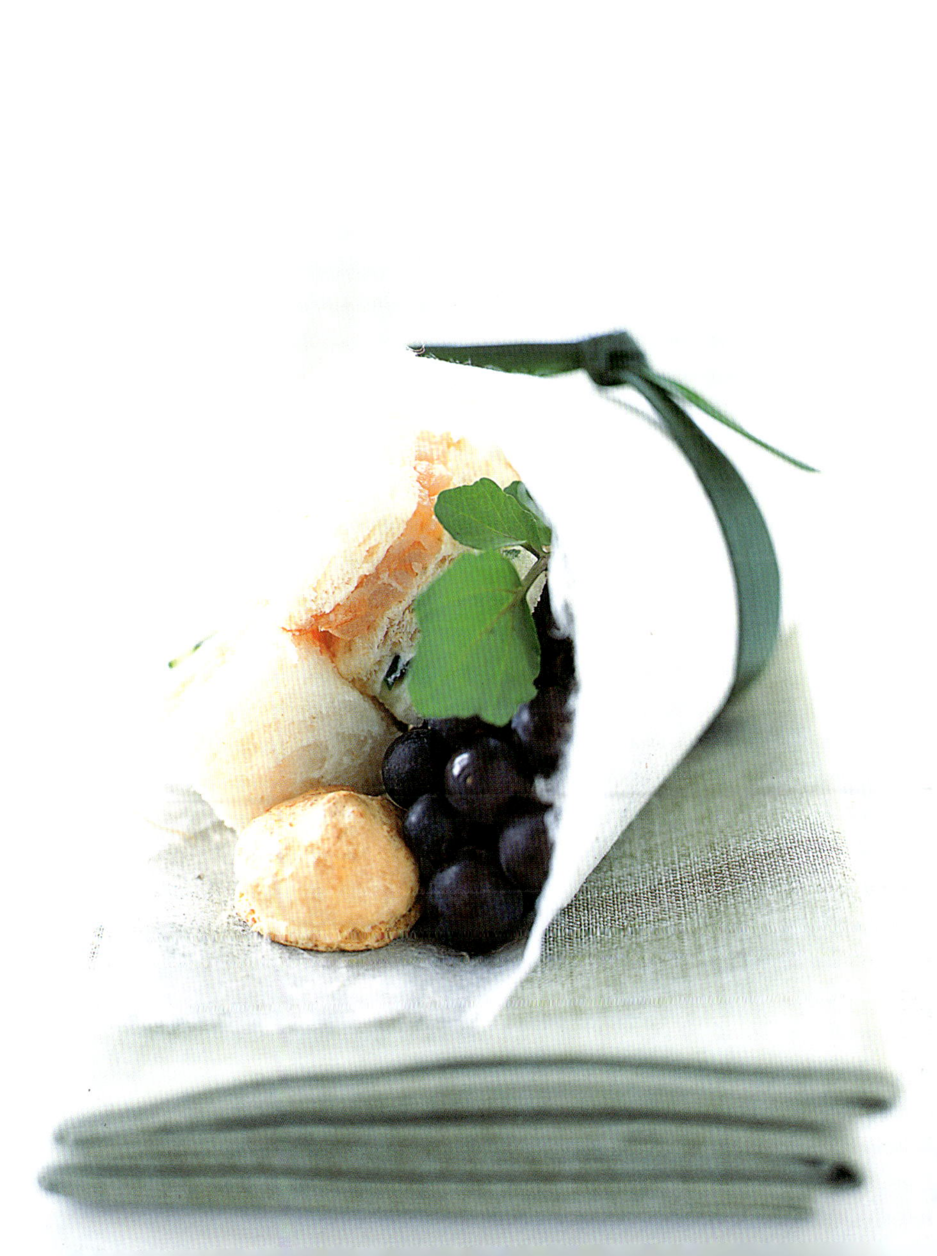

flowering pots

Small flowering plants like geraniums make wonderful decorations for outdoor tables. Group them together for maximum effect.

salad greens

Spring tables should be heaped with fresh produce. Crisp salad greens are cheap and tasty. Retain crunchiness by dressing at the last minute.

fresh colours

Cool greens and pretty pinks are perfect spring colours. Mix and match with white for a fresh, simple way to bring the new season to your table.

fantastic plastic

Plastic is a picnic essential. When china simply won't do, scout around for a good set of plastic plates and bowls in a luscious spring colour.

spring

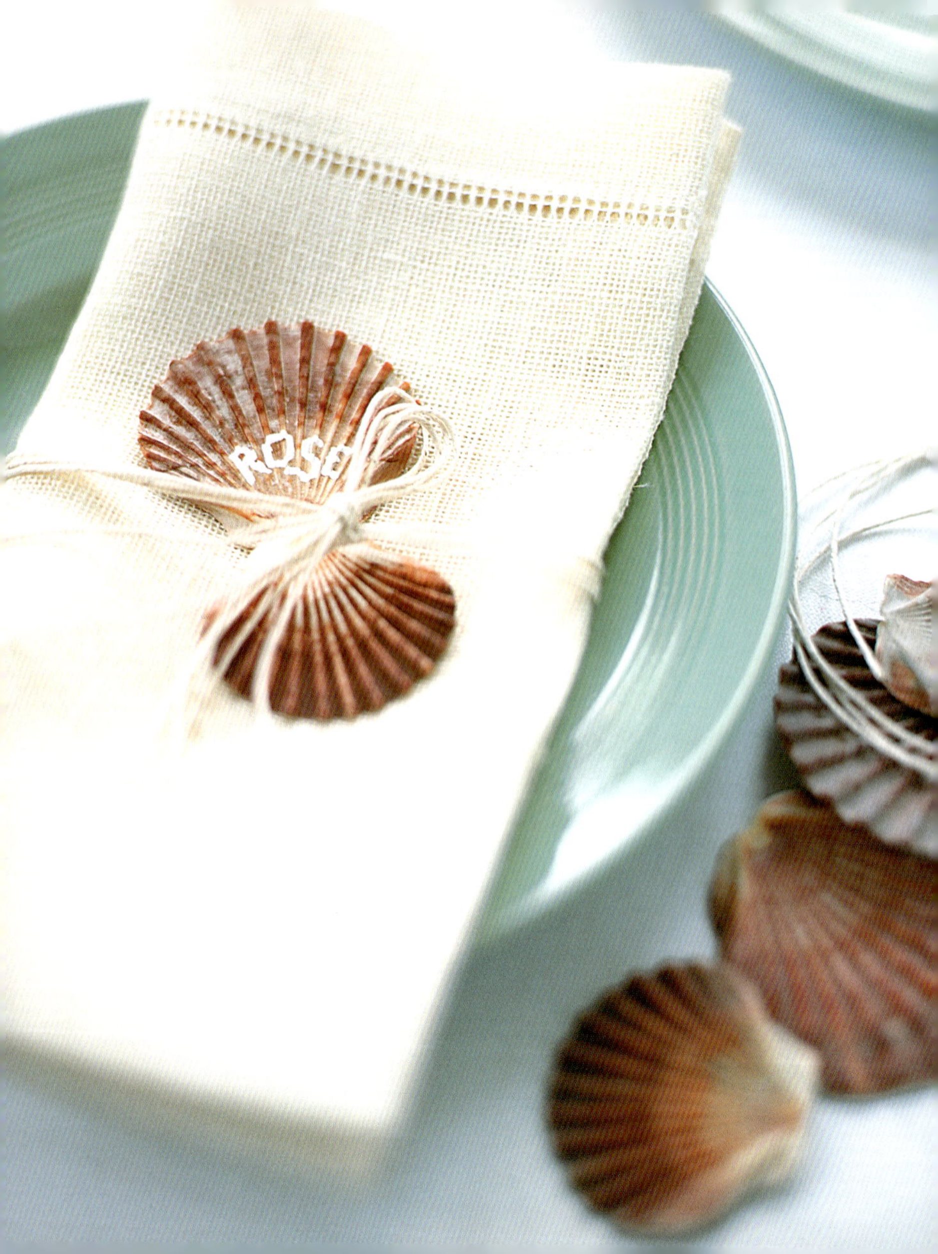
ROSE

break from tradition

Creating the perfect table at any time of the year is all about experimenting. It's about playing with colour and texture, being bold enough to break from tradition, using the beautiful and the bizarre. It's about big, bold statements and small, soft touches.

During spring, the formal and the informal can be mixed to great effect. Even if the occasion is a formal one—a wedding, a black-tie dinner—add a vibrant edge with some unusual or quirky elements. When it comes to setting the table, be adventurous. Use beautiful blossoms like hyacinths or primroses in small glass containers instead of vases. Add a little water to a ceramic bowl and fill with a mass of wonderful, fragrant spring blooms (just the flowers, not the stems). Don't be afraid to play with colour. Soft purples, pinks, greens and blues are striking when used either alone or together. Design and make simple yet elegant invitations and send them to your guests—they'll appreciate the time and effort you've put in. Leave formal napkin rings in their boxes and tie napkins with beautiful silk ribbons in delicious spring colours. Or collect some opened scallop shells and use them as name tags by writing the names of your guests on the shells in white pen. Then place the shells on top of your napkins. To finish them, tie with a length of white string.

Scallop shells double as place cards

garden treasures

Your garden may hold the key to a perfect spring table. A pair of gardening scissors and a small basket is all you need. When searching for flowers, collect blooms in the morning before the sun is at its highest. This ensures maximum longevity of your cut flowers.

Fill vases with fresh water and cut stems on a diagonal. Place in a cool area so that the blooms won't wilt. Collect a handful of glossy leaves or lavender flowers to use on your table.

Place lavender flowers on napkins and scatter the leaves at random over the table. Cut a few small, blossom-laden branches from fruit trees and arrange them in glass bottles or water glasses for a true touch of spring.

A line of leafy herb pots looks fantastic, smells wonderful and will add colour to the table. An inexpensive idea for a wedding or other romantic occasion is to transform small glass jam jars into beautiful lanterns by winding strands of ivy or jasmine around their openings. Secure the strands with glue or string so they won't unwind. Drop a candle into the jar and it's complete. Jars of differing types and sizes can all be used—group them together on a table or scatter them throughout the room. The perfume from the lavender and jasmine will delicately envelop the table with their sweet scents.

An old jar gets a new lease of life as a vine-wreathed candle holder

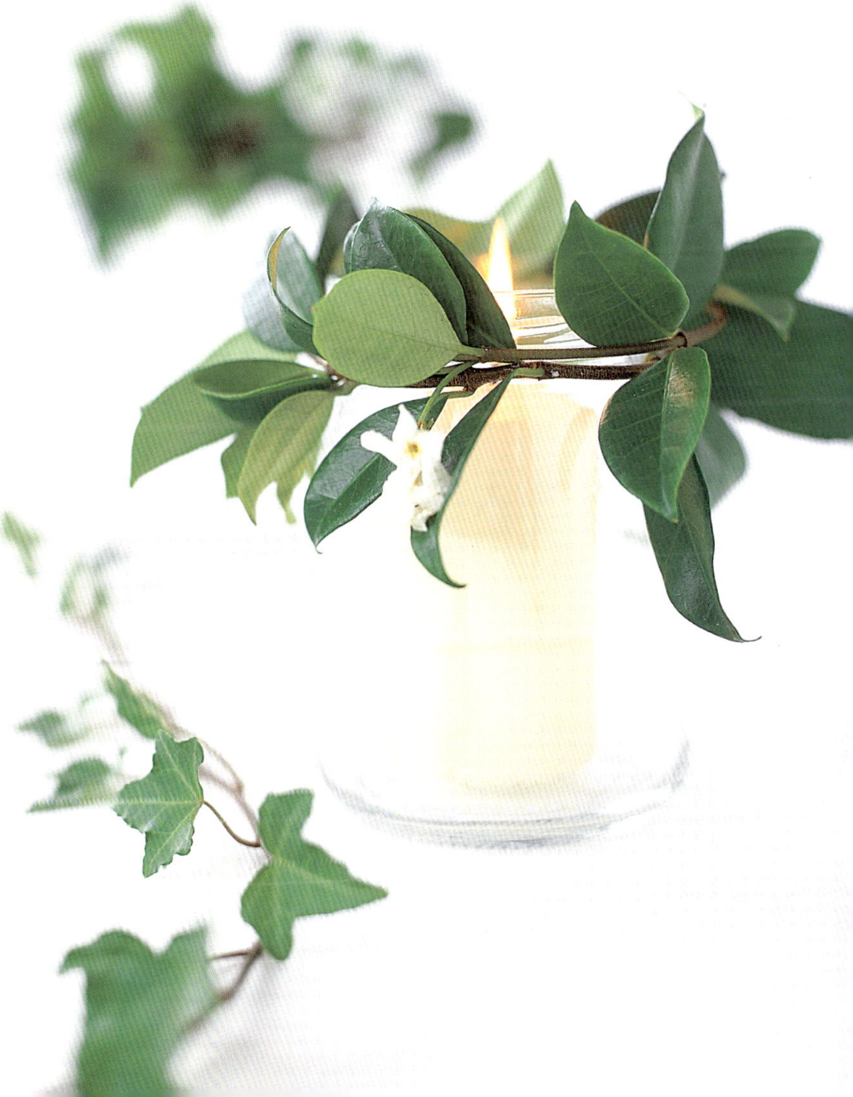

Published by Murdoch Books®,
a division of Murdoch Magazines Pty Ltd,
GPO Box 1203, Sydney, NSW Australia 2001.

Author: Karen Spresser
Stylist: Yael Grinham
Photographer: John-Paul Urizar
Concept & Design: Marylouise Brammer
Project Manager: Anna Waddington
Editor: Susan Gray

Chief Executive: Mark Smith
Publisher: Kay Scarlett
Production Manager: Liz Fitzgerald

National Library of Australia Cataloguing-in-Publication Data
Grinham, Yael.
Table.
ISBN 1 74045 088 4.
1. Table setting and decoration. I. Spresser, Karen. II. Urizar, John Paul. III. Title.
(Series: Marie Claire style.)
642.7

Printed by Toppan Printing Hong Kong Co. Ltd. PRINTED IN CHINA. First printed 2001.

© Text and design Murdoch Books® 2001. © Photography John-Paul Urizar 2001.
All rights reserved. No part of this publication may be reproduced, stored in any retrieval system or transmitted in any form or by any means, electronic, mechanical, photocopying, recording or otherwise, without the prior written permission of the publisher.
Murdoch Books® is a registered trademark of Murdoch Magazines Pty Ltd.